HIGHLY

SENSITIVE

PEOPLE

EMPATH, EMOTIONAL HEALING & CHAKRAS

By Melissa Anna Holloway

Main Table Of Contents

EMPATH

Empowering empaths,
healing, sensitive,
emotions, energy
& relationship

MELISSA A. HOLLOWAY

Empath:

Empowering empaths, healing, sensitive emotions, energy & relationships

By Melissa Anna Holloway

Empath : Table of Contents

Introduction

If you are an empath, know someone who is, or you are unsure about what the term means, then this book is for you. In the following chapters, I'll explain who is an empath and give you profound insight about certain attributes.

Moreover, if you are an empath, I will show you what you can do to embrace who you are and how to manage and organize your life so that it is more meaningful. If you know someone who is, it will give you a better understanding and appreciation of what empaths deal with on a daily basis.

An empath needs to pay close attention to his or her health. It is very crucial and significant. Living in this technological age is even more stressful for an empath than it was years before. This is because empaths are very sensitive to the electrical magnetic frequencies emitted by phone towers, mobile phones computers, and equipment found in the home such as the television and microwave. That is why great emphasis is placed not only on emotional and mental health, but also physical and spiritual health.

Attention is also placed on healing, and infusing positive energy and self-love. Empaths are by nature givers. Thus, there is need to replenish the body, mind, and soul to avoid fatigue and depression.

My wish for you is to enjoy life and have better relationships with friends, acquaintances, colleagues, and loved ones. It is time to pay attention to your needs and to understand that as an empath, you can live an inspiring and purposeful existence.

Chapter 1: Being an empath

An empath is someone who feels and is attuned to the sensation and emotions of other people. It is different than being sympathetic or being compassionate. An empath feels what others feel; the pain, suffering, depression, sadness, joy etc. It is not merely identifying with or reacting accordingly. It is to know and have the same sensations of other individuals.

Some empaths are also psychic. Many psychic empaths who have this gift choose to ignore it and do not tap into it. To differentiate an empath, the terminology 'average person' is used. It is in no way used to be off-putting but for the purposes of comparison.

There are different signs to ascertain if you are an empath. Let us examine them.

Detect what others feel

An empath knows what other people are experiencing. A person can say they are okay and all is well, but an empath knows the truth regardless of what someone says or tries to deny. The person does not have to be near. It doesn't have to be a friend or family member. It can be a stranger. An empath only needs to focus on the individual.

Empaths feel distressed when others are stressed and feel their suffering. It is not an act or a performance. It is just who they are.

Being sensitive in crowds

An empath has an intolerance and feels uneasy in noisy and overcrowded places such as night spots and shopping malls.

An average person can go to a nightclub or a party, have a few drinks and/or smoke. He or she can absorb the deafening music, dance to the beat and totally be comfortable in that environment.

Furthermore, an average person can visit the mall, either be in a hurry or just for leisure and feel normal. He can be preoccupied with many thoughts or be so absorbed in the spending thrift that he is not conscious about anything else.

An empath, let us refer to her as Cathy, can visit a shopping plaza and instantly her entire body will react. Her heart may race and her emotions fluctuate. The signs are akin to when someone is having a panic attack. Similarly, Cathy may go to a nightclub and try to tolerate the environment while secretly looking at her watch wanting to leave. As to not appear dull and boring, she does her best to deal with it while feeling quite uncomfortable.

Depression

Clinical depression affects many people around the world. Empaths are vulnerable and more prone because of how they are wired. Compare to the average person, empaths take matters more personally.

The depression may be an accumu
trauma that an empath has encountered
throughout the years. To deal with it, an empath
who doesn't know what is happening or that he
is an empath may ignore and block certain
feelings which result in depression.

An overpowering feeling of guilt

An empath genuinely cares about people and
will do what they can to make others happy.
However, when something terrible happens
empaths perceive the situation as not doing all
that was necessary to prevent it from
happening. They feel as if they are to be blamed
for whatever transpired.

On the other hand, if someone took their advice
but didn't implement it properly, an empath
may feel it is his fault. Even when there is

nothing an empath can do to help a situation; an empath will somehow feel responsible.

Let us use this example. Tom has a successful marriage and shared advice with his friend Andy on what he needs to do to create a blissful marriage. Tom is not a psychic empath. What Tom doesn't know is that Andy's wife wants a divorce and has communicated it to Andy. Andy doesn't tell this to Tom for then he would have to reveal the reason his wife wants to leave him. The reason is that Andy has been physically abusive. Tom hears about the divorce from other friends. Tom somehow feels that he didn't do enough to help Andy save his marriage. Tom mulls over the situation and blames himself for not expressing himself better or being more helpful as a friend.

Oversensitivity

Normally, when someone's presence is not welcomed, an average person may not know. For those who are aware he or she may choose to ignore what is happening or leave without any hard feelings.

Empath on the other hand are very sensitive when their presence is not wanted. This situation can be traced back to childhood. For example, perhaps these empaths who are highly intuitive when their presence isn't needed, didn't have close friends, or were unpopular. They may have deflected it by being part of groups but not overstaying their welcome. Others may apologize profusely for intruding.

Nonetheless, popular empaths can also sense rejection too. It is just that for empaths who weren't as popular, the feeling is more pronounced for them.

The benefit of the doubt

As mentioned before, empaths suffer from guilt. Empaths do not like to hurt other people. If someone has wrong them, empaths will quicker choose to give someone another chance or chances than an average person. They want to be sure that their next step is the best move. They rationalize what someone did. They may think: *Perhaps the person is having a tough time. Perhaps the person is ill. Perhaps I should adjust rather than confront what the other person has done.*

The average person will react but an empath will be at a standstill first and contemplate his options.

When empaths are giving people more chances and giving the benefit of the doubt, the perpetrator is viewing them as being weak. Others may view them as foolish and being taken advantage of. Am empath needs to know when enough is enough and be guided to trust their own instinct.

Feeling like you do not fit in

If you are not an empath but ever listen to empaths speak, they often express that they feel like they do not fit in or they feel weird around others. If you are an empath, you often feel this way. This is because an empath has realized that his level of sensitivity and awareness is more heightened than others. When empaths do not have someone to reason with or share what they feel, they often feel alone.

A more advanced empath, has come to terms with his gift and understand when others may view them as being peculiar or in a strange manner. A more experienced empath knows that it is not everyone who can understand how they are.

A connection with the surroundings

An empath can feel the energy from the type of environment. It can be an open space, or there can be houses all around. When looking for a house, an empath knows which place is just right.

An empath does not need to be living in a place to know when something is right or wrong, as he or she can detect it. For example, an average person who is house hunting will select a home based on the cost, the proximity, the neighborhood etc. An empath will make a selection based on the vibrations. For example, when he feels uneasy, skin gets goose chills or if he feels tension in a room. No matter how great the price is or how lovely are the surroundings, once an empath picks up bad energy, he knows that something is wrong.

On the other hand, the surrounding may not be the best pick for an average person and the price may be too costly, but once an empath feels a good energy that is what matters.

Always helping

An empath can't resist reaching out and helping others. The first impulse is to help. An experienced empath knows when to set boundaries, when to help and when to move on. Helping is not for simple tasks like opening the door, holding the elevator, or saying thank you. Human beings can choose to be polite or impolite.

An empath will go overboard. They will give their last meal or last dollar. They frequently put themselves last and others first. Once others are happy, they are happy; never mind they are drained and exhausted. An empath must learn how to manage this trait or it can lead to resentment and depression.

Have an awareness to detect when being lied to or being deceived

An empath knows when something is wrong. It doesn't happen automatically as some empaths operate on different levels. An empath who has more experience can read the signs well. As humans, we all can know when something is amiss. However, an empath goes much deeper and can sense another person's intention.

Sometimes, it will take time to figure out what exactly is happening. However, an empath knows that is something is occurring but may not know what exactly.

As mentioned earlier an empath likes to give others the benefit of the doubt. So, though he may be aware that something is amiss, he will wait to see if the person has a change of heart or may do the right thing.

Even when someone thinks that he or she has fooled an empath, eventually an empath will know what is going on once the empath pays attention to how they are feeling and what is being sensed.

Being overwhelmed

When too many things are occurring at once or there are many individuals around an empath, he or she will feel burdened. As an empath picks up energies, at some point they will feel overwhelmed.

Feeling anxious

Empaths have a tendency to suffer with anxiety.

Healing capabilities

Empaths can send healing to others or they can place their hands on other people and make them feel better. An advanced empath can participate in remote healing, psychic healing and saying prayers that heal.

Chapter 2: Coping Tips to Help You Embrace Your Gift

In our previous chapter, we discussed certain signs to know if you're an empath. Here, I will share with you what you can do to cope with your gift in the same order as we outlined for the signs.

Set boundaries

As empaths know what others feel, it is very crucial that empaths maintain boundaries. You do not necessarily have to have rigid rules about interacting with your friends. However, you must keep boundaries and ask your friends to respect them.

Let's assume that Cathy is a consultant and works from home. Her friends especially her needy friends pop in anytime. The needy ones unburden their problems on her for over an hour and the more they feel at ease, the more Cathy feels burdened and depressed. It has gotten to such a point where Cathy is unable to concentrate properly after they leave and it interferes with her productivity.

Boundaries include informing friends when you won't be available to commiserate with them. Or it can be as simple as asking them to call before popping in unannounced.

Another boundary is to set limits. It is not that you are not available to talk but one hour and two hours are very taxing on an empath. You can invite a group of friends so that rather than the needy friend draining your reserves, other friends with positive energy can keep your energy levels up.

Avoid drugs and excessive alcohol drinking when in crowded environment
Empaths find it hard to be in huge crowds or at loud parties. To stabilize the energy, avoid using drugs and alcohol.

There are some empaths who use alcohol and drugs as a form of escapism from what they are feeling and their reality. They do not know how to cope or they may not even understand the gifting they have and what is happening so they use the substances as a crutch. These are but temporary solutions as after the effect has worn off, the situation remains.

An empath must also realize that drugs and alcohol make you even more susceptible to surrounding energies. You won't be as alert as you should be. You won't be able to concentrate and your movements will be inhibited.

Let's assume that Cathy is walking home from a party and she feels weird. Cathy may assume that it's the effect of the substance consumed when in reality there may be an impending danger.

If you consume it in your leisure time, it's up your choice. However, when you are already sensitive to crowds and noise, it is more devastating for you create more harm by interfering with your energy levels. If you have to visit a mall choose a day when it is not as busy.

Understanding the root cause of a problem

Depending on what is the root cause of a situation, it may take a long time to resolve it or find a solution. However, if anxiety one of your main symptoms, one way to combat it is to take time to figure out what is causing the problem.

For example, perhaps every time you visit a relative you get anxiety attacks. What about this relative is causing you to react this way? Does this stem from something that happened in your childhood? Is this relative manipulative or abusive in some way? Why do you keep going if you feel this way? Is there an emotional tie to this individual?

If you cannot shirk that responsibility for example the person is ill, then visit the relative with someone else to help you get through that tough period. Take another relative with you who calms you or ask a friend to accompany you.

Understand that you are not responsible for what others do

Empaths want to save everyone. It is best to come to the realization that you have to save yourself in order to be helpful to anyone. One way of saving yourself is not take responsibilities for matters which you are not responsible for. In our example of Tom and Andy, Tom needs to understand that he is not responsible for anything.

Every human being has a level of consciousness. Human beings have the ability to learn from their mistakes and do better. You are not with other people 24/7. You cannot control them. Therefore, empaths must find a way to stop carrying around so much guilt. If you advised someone and they didn't take your advice, and failed, there is nothing else you could have done. Or if they took your advice and things didn't work out how you expected, realize that it is part of life. Once you have no ulterior motives and you genuinely wanted the best for that individual, do not wallow in sadness until eternity. There are other people who you can be of help to, but you will never progress if you let one incident inhibit your progress.

Change your perspective

Empaths are highly sensitive when their presence is not welcomed. Others may pretend or try to mask how they really feel but an empath knows otherwise. To combat this, change your perspective entirely. Yes, you are different.

However, just like when sometimes you do not understand what you are feeling or what message the universe is sending you, similarly others may not understand you. Your light may be too bright for them. Do not take it personally. It's hard not to especially when you think highly of the person or it's a close friend.

Respect yourself enough by discontinuing the habit of trying to fit in. When you accept who you are, you will attract the right people who accept you and enjoy your company. You will never reach to this level though, if you keep going to places where you are not wanted.

The minute you keep apologizing for who you are, it means that you need to assess the situation from another angle. Respect yourself enough to honor who you.

This coping mechanism also relates to the heading "Feeling like you do not fit in", Connection to the surroundings" and "Awareness to detect when being lied to or being deceived." The more you accept your gifting, the less fear and anxiety you will have.

Trust the energy

An empath who has just become aware of who he or she is, will give people the benefit of the doubt more often than a more experienced empath. Experience will guide you when it's time to break free from a situation or someone. You should trust your energy level more. Even if the person has an attractive face, smiles but telling you a string of lies that someone else may not know about, if you feel that they are deceptive, trust your instinct.

Vibrations

There are various levels of vibrations. Some things create harmony and others disharmony. One way to cope is knowing what gives you harmony and how you can align yourself more with this energy.

The land and your surrounding has a vibration. When selecting a home, ensure that you choose one where you feel a sense of calm. Your home is where you should feel safe and secure, the place that shields you from the rest of the world. It makes no sense to be in an environment that leaves you distressed and then still have to deal with stressful situations outside the home. Make sure you feel at peace where you reside.

If the situation is such that you cannot relocate or move, find objects or furniture that can balance the energy inside of your home.

Color

There are some colors that you are more drawn too. You feel more self-assured and stronger every time you wear a particular color. As you advance on your journey, you will realize that colors have more impact for empaths.

Clothes

Wearing clothes, is more than paying attention to the color. It also pertains to the style and how it fits you. An empath must pay attention to what is worn as it will affect your mood. If you have to attend a function in an environment that you do not like, it is important that you feel your best. Wear something that will sustain your energy level.

Gemstones

Gemstones, crystals, and rocks have a vibration. They can alter your mood. You have to know which ones are best for you. Feel it to determine your energy level. Some may tingle in your hand others may do absolutely nothing for you. Others may give you a peace of mind and soothe your soul. Know what works best for you and keep it close.

Meditation

Meditating and expressing certain mantras can dissolve bad energy and infuse your spirit with good energy. It is not just saying them for the sake of saying but it must believe in what you are expressing.

As an empath, you must be cognizant that your thoughts also have a vibration. Reflect on what you are thinking and saying and make sure they are in harmony with what you truly want. Ask your friends to point out to you when you have uttered negative comments or you're saying things not in keeping with what you are hoping for.

Flower Remedies

Plants and flowers have vibrations. We discuss this in one of our chapters.

Chapter 3: Grounding

Grounding is the term given to defuse negative energies and infuse yourself with positive energy.

Water

Water is a vital component of life. Some empaths are grounded when immersed in water. In fact, some visualize water and use the mental imagery to calm them when in a distressing situation and they cannot be close to water. If there was a way to walk around with showers the same way we do our cell phones, empaths would be the first to have them. Water not only cleanses the body from dirt but it has healing powers and removes negative energy.

Food

Food plays a significant role for empaths. Food has energy. If this is said to the average person, he or she may look at you like a peculiar person but many empaths know this. Some empaths know when food was prepared with someone with negative energy or someone in a foul mood. Without even tasting it, an experienced empath knows when something shouldn't be eaten. An empath who is in tune with him or herself will know from the vibrations when something isn't right.

With the advancement of technology more information is coming to light to the public about the harmful effects of chemicals that are used on food. There are countless articles about hormones being used on livestock to make them grow faster and look fatter. More people are getting sick, damaging their bodies, and depriving their bodies of valuable nutrients and minerals by what they eat. When we eat the wrong food, it harms the body. For an empath, food preparation and eating is even more magnified.

Foods affect your hormones, mood swings, and level of sensitivity. What you eat also affects how you respond to people's energy. If you are going through a rough time and have assumed that the problem is psychological or emotional yet you cannot figure out what it is you need to do to get better, change your diet. The positive results will astound you.

Burning herbs, incense and using smoke
This is referred to as smudging and is used by individuals to clear negative environment. We're aware that Native Indians years ago, used smoke in their healing ceremonies. Today this practice is still very dominant in certain countries.

Select an aroma that you prefer if you engage in this practice.

Herbs that are frequently used include cedar, lavender, sage and sweetgrass.

If you will be cleansing your home, let the smoke float from the floor up to the roof. Don't forget the corners of your home where negative energy may be. If you have smoke alarms be mindful of how you are cleansing your home.

If you are clearing bad energy from items, put the item in the way of the smoke until you sense the negativity has been cleared.

If you are cleaning your body, work from your feet upwards and come up over your head. Do the front, back and sides. Include under your feet and under the arms. Remember to put out any burning substance or incense when you are not at home.

Exercise

For an empath, there is more to exercise than losing weight. Exercise is a way to release negative vibrations. Choose the form of exercise that suits you. If you like routine then stick to a schedule but if you exercise when you feel like it, do so. Exercise also improves your mood and overall feeling.

Meditation

In today's world, there is too much noise. Horns blowing, pings and calls from phones, television in the background, neighbor blasting a stereo, children screaming, bosses nagging, coworkers chattering and the dog barking. Added to this, is are the thoughts in your mind. Your fears and anxieties coupled with other people's emotions will burden you. Meditation is important. It stills a busy mind and relaxes the body. During the time of meditation, it helps you to sift through and discard what you do not need to concentrate on. It also helps you to separate your thoughts from other people thoughts.

Have an outlet

Whether it's painting, dancing, baking, cooking, drawing, making craft or gardening, every empath should engage in an activity other than work and home related activities. Find an interest that you enjoy doing. It enhances your mood and is a great way to inject positivity in your life.

Nature

The great outdoors has healing properties for an empath. Take time to enjoy nature. If you are not fortunate to live close to a park or natural environment, schedule in your planner when you will go somewhere to enjoy nature. It can be after work, before work, or on weekends.

Walk barefoot

This is also referred to as earthing. Have you ever felt like you are a live wire? There are electrical magnetic frequencies all around you, such as from mobile phones, television, and computers. So, next time you feel wired, walk barefoot when it is safe to do so.

Some empaths ensure that when they sleep, cell phones are a distance away and the television and computers are shut off because they pick up the frequencies.

Oils

Aromatherapy is important for an empath. It helps with relaxation. We will discuss this in a separate chapter.

Gemstones and Crystals

Gemstones and crystals also help empaths to stay grounded. There is a separate chapter on this.

Chapter 4: Shielding

For an empath, shielding is a way to decrease negative energy and maintain your energy level. This is important especially when interacting with stressful and demanding people and when empaths are in an environment that is noisy or uncomfortable.

Visualization

Use imagery to channel your energy. You can imagine an impenetrable bubble around you or a cloak. Or you can use both imagery of a cloak and bubble. Cover yourself with a cloak and then surround yourself with your personalized bubble. The color of the bubble can be your favorite color and you can add an extra layer by surrounding yourself with a white bubble.

When you are cloaking yourself, you can use an invisible cloak, smoke cloak or one that reflects like a mirror. You will know from experience the different type of cloaks to work with. Individuals may perceive you differently so know when to use which cloak when interacting with someone or when in a particular environment.

Crystals and Oils

Like grounding, crystal and oils are also used for shielding. You can incorporate your gemstone or crystal in your jewelry. Or you can carry it in your pocket or purse.

Communicate Effectively

You are wired to help. Even when something will take much out of you and you are on the brink of collapse, empaths struggle with letting people know when enough is enough. You must learn to help YOURSELF and one way to do so is by learning how to be effective when communicating. You can let someone know you are not available in many ways. For example, it is fine to say any of these phrases: *I need to rest.*

I have other plans. I can recommend you to someone. You can read more about this. Feel free to send an email as I am unable to visit. I am working overtime.

Also, you must communicate your needs. You may be able to know what others want but that doesn't mean that they can. So, learn to express what you want from others rather than hope and wish that they will do something or say something.

Someone may think of the word garbage. An empath may know that they are thinking that the garbage needs to be taken outside. Before they can even say anything, an empath will offer to take it outside. When it is an empath's turn, he may put the garbage in front of the door and someone may step right over it. If you're an empath, the lesson is, don't assume anything. Learn to ask people to do things. Simply express, *"Please take out the garbage."* Be cognizant that you are in a low percentage when compared to the rest of the population. Therefore, don't assume that people will know what you want. Say what you want or write what you want to be done by leaving a note.

Boundaries

Previously, we explored the importance of boundaries when highlighting ways to manage. It is also a shielding method. There is a reason why there are doors on buildings, and gates and fences in a yard. It is to prevent trespassers and for protection. Likewise, not only must you protect your physical space, but also your emotional, energetic, and mental space.

Chapter 5: Essential Oils

Not every oil should be used on skin. Moreover, for certain oils which can be used on the skin, individuals with sensitive and damaged skin must be aware of the effect the oil may have. Skin conditions may develop and for people with damaged skin, it may cause the condition to worsen.

Oils are usually concentrated. Therefore a few drops can be used. Some of the oils which are classed as irritants as they have an immediate effect when applied to skin include: clove bud, citronella, cinnamon bark or leaf and bay oil.

You can mix essential oils with a base oil such as almond oil, olive oil, or grapeseed oil. A base oil is also referred to as a carrier oil and it is used for dilution. For oils which cannot be used on the skin, you can use them as aerosol sprays.

Other oils can be inhaled from the container, or applied to a fabric to inhale. If you have respiratory problems be very mindful of what oils you are inhaling. It is always good to test by spraying a little mist in the environment first and see how you react to it. If you are pregnant be very vigilant with how you use various oils. If you are unsure consult a health professional.

Some oils can also be ingested. Make sure that when purchasing them you read all labels and directions carefully.

I wish to share with you some of the oils you can use and when is the best time to use them.

Basil
Basil is great for cooking. As an oil, it is very uplifting and enhances your mood. It is ideal to use when feeling anxious, tired, or depressed. Mental concentration also improves after usage.

It is also consumed as a digestive tonic. The oil mixes well with other oils such as rosemary, neroli, clary sage, eucalyptus, and geranium.

Chamomile

Chamomile is famously known for its sedative qualities. As a tea, it is good for relaxation purposes. It also aids with balancing hormones. You can place a few drops of the oil on your pillow or add it to the bath water.

Frankincense

It is great for clearing the mind when you feel burdened with many thoughts. It is used in many religions. Several sources indicate that it stimulates the brain's limbic system. The limbic system is the part of the brain that influences your emotional wellbeing. In addition, part of the system aids in developing and preserving memories.

When buying, make sure you are selecting the essential oil and not a watered-down version that says perfume oil.

One of the reasons why it is used in religious practices, is because it induces a peaceful atmosphere. If you are stressed, include a few drops in your bath for relaxation or you can vaporize the atmosphere.

Some individuals use it when meditating and claim that it enhances spiritual connection.

If you suffer from pain and inflammation, you can massage with it and it helps your circulation. Alternatively, you can steam water, add a few drops, immerse a towel in the water and put the towel on the specific part of the body that is in pain.

It can be used as an aid for sleeping as well and it mixes well with lavender oil.

Geranium

It is a sedative and it can also uplift your mood. It also enhances your mental clarity. Geranium is called the poor man's rose as this oil and rose oil share comparable traits but this is cheaper.

It also aids in reducing inflammation and pain. The oil can be used in baked goods and beverages.

Jasmine

This oil improves a person's mood and it is also an aphrodisiac. It invigorates and release serotonin hormones in the body and arouses your sensual desire. In certain cultures, the flowers are used to adorn brides. It can be used to improve your sleep also.

Lavender

It clears the mind, relaxes the body, and eliminates negative energy. It is used to alleviate stress, migraines, and depression. It is documented that people who have migraines, use lavender oil to lessen the pain. Individuals also mix it with peppermint oil, to combat headaches.

Neroli

If you are going to a busy or noisy place and will feel overwhelmed, carry a bit of neroli oil with you. It balances the mood and it is used to counter anxiety and hysteria. It is also helps with sleeping.

Clary Sage

The word clary in Latin means cleansing or clarifying. It is a milder version of sage oil and has a sweet smell. It eases anxiety, calms the nervous system, and balances your hormones.

You can dilute it with a carrier oil and pour a few drops to your bath water.

Sage

Sage oil is stronger and has a spice scent. It reduces inflammation and balance hormones. It needs to be diluted with a carrier oil.

When you need an upliftment in your mood and to dissipate mental fatigue, sage oil can be used. It blends well with clary sage, geranium, and lavender.

Rose oil

This oil improves your confidence and mental prowess. It is also great to combat depression. Using this oil will induce positive thinking, spiritual rest, and happiness. This oil is also used as an aphrodisiac and invokes romantic emotions.

Sandalwood

The woodsy smell of sandalwood oil positively affects the brain. If you need to boost your memory, this oil should be used. In addition, it has a calming effect when a person is experiencing depression, fear, stress, or anxiety. It mixes well with rose, lavender and geranium. You can use it when meditating, praying and for other spiritual routines.

Eucalyptus

When you are mentally tired, exhausted, feeling nauseous, or ill this oil can revitalize you. The flow of blood is improved after usage. Therefore, it is ideal to stimulate your mind.

You can massage the body with it when you have muscle pain. If there is a patient in a room, you can use it to freshen the room and sterilize the environment as it eradicates bacteria and germs.

In spas and saunas, the oil is used for its refreshing attributes.

Peppermint oil

A few drops of this oil in beverages helps with digestion. It is used for empaths who have no appetite, feel nauseous, suffer with headaches, or have an upset stomach.

It is used to eliminate depression, stress, and anxiety.

Storage

Ensure that bottles are properly closed and stored in a cool place. They should not be in sunlight or be close to flammable materials. Make sure that oils are not placed where children or pets can reach them.

Chapter 6: Flower Remedies

Flower Remedies, are the popular term but the official term is Bach Flower Remedies. The name is derived from Dr. Edward Bach, a British doctor who in his experimentation observed that different plants have an effect on an individual's emotions. He dedicated his time to finding natural solutions for common problems as opposed to prescribing man-made drugs that doctors regularly recommend.

They are produced by adding flowers to water and leaving them in the sunshine for a few hours. The other alternative is to boil the flowers in a pot. There are procedures which must be followed so it is best to purchase them rather than experimenting, if you a novice. If you prefer to make them, study the process and be very versed in what you are doing before ingesting them. The authentic remedies have a Bach label on the bottles with the instructions. You can find them in health stores and pharmacies.

The mixture is preserved with brandy. If you do not wish to use it because of the alcohol, you can dilute it or place a few drops on your wrist and temple. For an empath who understand how nature works, these flower remedies, are filled with the vibration of plants and flowers.

Rock Rose

This is referred to as an emergency remedy. It is applied when someone needs rescuing in cases of an incident, poor health, or someone is terribly scared. For example, when a place is haunted or something foul is around, this can be used.

Mimulus

When someone has fears, this remedy is used to conquer them. For example, if you are afraid of heights, fear rejection or fear a particular bug, keep this close. As mentioned before, some empaths struggle with trying to fit in. For those who do, this remedy will play a significant role.

Cherry Plum

Some empaths try and suppress their emotions, some are cynical and others have much anxiety. They may also have intense or violently behaviorisms. Cherry Plum will help empaths to be more expressive without the negative energy.

Aspen

When there are messages but you are not deciphering them well and you feel like imminent doom is about to take place, Aspen should be used. If you often walk around feeling good one minute and then suddenly there is dread all around you and you have no idea where it comes from, this remedy helps.

Red chestnut

Red chestnut is the remedy to use if you frequently worry about someone. If there is a friend or family member you usually visit but every time you feel anxious around him or her, carry red chestnut with you.

Cerato

As an empath, you may seek advice. However, there are certain matters that you should make decisions on your own as you are more aware than the average human being. When you are less self-assured and not confident, yet there is need to make a decision, this remedy should be used.

Scleranthus

If it feels like you are unable to make up your mind, one time you feel a certain way is correct and seconds later you feel that it's wrong, scleranthus will help you choose. It aids empaths who are indecisive.

Gentian

Are you disheartened? Has something delayed your progress and now you are dispirited? If so keep gentian close and use it to pull you through those tough times.

Gorse

A feeling of uselessness and despair can be remedied with gorse. After usage, you will feel hopeful again.

Hornbeam

Use hornbeam if you are feeling burdened and weak. It doesn't have to be your entire body but it can also be a part of your body that needs strength.

Impatiens

Some empaths are swift in how they think and act. They want stuff to be completed without any interruption or postponement. When this person is sick, anxiety is prevalent. It is hard for them to be patient especially with people who move slowly and take their dear own time to finish certain tasks. For those who fall in this category, this flower remedy is prescribed.

Heather

Many people are lonely and in search for company and friendship. These individuals are afraid of being by themselves as they do not like their own company. They dread being alone. When in the company of others they talk a lot and it is hard for others to get to interrupt them. An empath who has to deal with these type of people should consider used this flower remedy. Also, if the empath has this type of personality, they should also use this flower remedy.

Wild Oat

If you are very ambitious, know you want to do someone of distinction and have a rewarding career, use wild oat.

For Dreamy People

Clematis

If your present circumstances do not appeal to you and you fondly look forward to the future, use this remedy.

Honeysuckle

Do you live in the past? Are you nostalgic for what happened years ago, as they were happier times? To help you with your present situation, honeysuckle can be used.

Wild Rose

For empaths who go through the motions of life without being happy or feeling fulfilled, wild rose is the answer.

Olive

Feeling mentally or physically exhausted? Do you have to exert yourself a lot just to get by? Olive remedy will improve the feeling.

White Chestnut

For empaths who are bombarded with thoughts and quarrels, and they take up much space in their minds, white chestnut is the answer. No longer should negativity permanently reside in your mind. You should have peaceful thoughts.

Mustard

Empaths who feel as if their lives are filled with gloom and doom and it is like a dark cloud is over their heads, mustard is the remedy.

Oversensitive

Agrimony

Empaths understand that sharing with others how they truly feel, will cause them to be viewed peculiarly or being labelled as weird. Many empaths know it is best to keep their thoughts to themselves, unless they have a confidante.

Some empaths have mastered the art of putting on a brave front frequently responding that all is well. The truth for many is that they feel tormented and are very unhappy inside. Agrimony helps this type of empath to overcome the habit of hiding how they really feel.

Centaury

For individuals, always willing to be of service to others and go the extra mile, centaury helps to keep them balanced. Service at times can be read as an easy walk over and people can treat you like a doormat. Centaury brings clarity. The empath can know when they are being manipulated because of their kind heartedness. It protects empaths from being abused and give them the assertiveness to express when enough is enough.

Vexing Thoughts

Holly

Empaths are peaceful people. Yet they are human. This remedy helps empaths who are plagued with jealousy, distrust, vexing and vindictive thoughts from time to time.

Blameworthiness

Pine

Use this remedy if you are in the habit of blaming yourself and take responsibility for the errors people make when actually it is not your fault.

Chapter 7: Meditation

Every person should make time to meditate. However, many don't. On the other hand, as an empath, it should not be an option that is used as a last resort but should be scheduled regularly as a matter of necessity. To live a more enriching and balanced life, it is vital.

Earlier, we mentioned that exercise is a way to release negative vibrations. It is also a way to strengthen your resolve as you will have more positive energy. If you have a regular routine, you know how powerful exercise is. Similarly, the brain needs to be strengthened and you can do so by meditation.

Meditation is about being aware. It is more than thinking and wondering. Some individuals are of the view that meditation is about thinking and reflecting on something. As a result, people say that they engage in meditation when they are actually not doing so for while thinking they are multitasking, very active and being bombarded with distressing thoughts and focusing on them.

Examples of meditation:

Zen Meditation

With this type of meditation attention is placed on one's position. Your eyes need to be focused on a single feature. This meditation is ideal for individuals whose imagination takes them all the over place when they close their eyes. Proper posture and regular routine is necessary to be successful with this type of meditation

With this method, you are focusing on the *now* instead of the past or future. Your mind should not wander. Your facial muscles should be relaxed.

There are different ways to do this. The customary way is to sit in what is called the lotus position. However, that is the traditional way and you can have a posture that is more comfortable for you.

This is a simple way. Choose a posture that you can endure easily for a few minutes. For example, you can sit or kneel on a bench or cushion or sit in a chair. Center your spine and let your shoulders relax. Align your nose with your navel and make sure your head is straight.

Your head should not be leaning forward, sideways, or backwards. Place your hands on your thighs or lap comfortably. Place your left hand on top of your right hand with both palms facing upwards. Keep your lips closed and inhale through you nose filling your abdomen with the oxygen then release the air slowly. As you inhale count that as one, when you breathe out count that as two, breathing in again is three continuing with that rhythm for a few counts.

You will notice that thoughts will come to you and you may experience certain feelings but do not stop the meditation. It is like you are on a plane and your thoughts are like clouds floating by. You notice them but you surely don't shout and scream when you see the clouds. Similarly, thoughts will come but let them float by. The more you meditate, the more you will be accustomed to the process.

Loving Kindness Meditation

This type of meditation is very helpful for empaths who constantly blame themselves and struggle with feelings of guilt and blameworthiness. This meditation is coupled with words of affirmation to invoke positive and loving energy.

A simple way to do this is to get comfortable and relaxed. Inhale and when exhaling take a long time to get the air out. As you exhale, release anything that you have been focusing on. Then show love first to yourself. Empaths are so busy giving their all to everyone, that they are left feeling depleted. So, repeat words of affirmation like:

May I be cheerful. May I be safe. May I be well. May I be at peace.
As you say them, mean them, and feel them. Let the words wash over you like cleansing water.

You can combine this with visualization exercises. Have a mental picture of yourself looking happy and at peace.

If you are using essential oils that will awaken the senses or burning incense while saying this, you will have an ultimate experience.

After saying your affirming words to yourself, you can then focus on others. Concentrate on a friend and say the words to send them happiness and peace. Then say it to someone you find it difficult to work with. The next step is to send the energy to everyone: yourself, your friend or acquaintance and the person who is difficult.

There is no word that is set in stone. You can add your own words but make sure the words give you a warm feeling. During this type of meditation, adverse emotions such as grief and anger may arise. Do not get scared and stop. What is happening is that all the negative emotions are coming to the surface. Let the negative energy flow up and out of your being. Replace that unwanted emotions with love.

Mantra Meditation

With mantra meditation, the mind is focused by expressing a word or words. It is like digging underground, rather than focusing on the earth surface. I use the analogy of digging for that is what you are doing to your mind. You are planting positive seeds in your mind but to do this, you have to dig below the surface. You are removing the negative vibrations and replacing it with powerful vibrations.

Words that can be used:

- Om or Aum when translated means "to become" or "it is."

- Be the change you wish to see in the world - Gandhi
- Sat Chit Ananda meaning "existence, consciousness, bliss."
- I change my thoughts I change my world –quote from Norman Vincent Peale
- I am that I am – God's response to Moses
- El Shaddai meaning God Almighty

Christian Meditation

This type of mediation is for the purpose of being closer to Christ/God.

Forms include

- prayer and devotions
- contemplative reading – the bible or spiritual text is read to get a deeper understanding of the teachings of Christ and how God operates

•   spending time with God –the focus is on God's will for the empath's life and exercising faith as oppose to focusing on fear and doom

There are various forms of meditation. These were listed to show that every religion has its own way of doing things. If you are not a religious person, or do not consider yourself as 'spiritual,' at the end of the day, choose a form of meditation that will give you inner peace. Use whichever form of meditation works best for you.

Benefits of meditation
- Helps combat depression
- Regulate mood swings
- Diminishes anxiety, panic, and stress
- Minimizes your reliance on drugs and alcohol
- Helps you to concentrate better

Chapter 8: Gemstones and Crystals

Empaths are labelled with many names by people who do not understand how burdensome it can get at times. Empaths need to know how to protect themselves and the importance of using several ways and methods to have more balance and peace in their lives.

Gemstones revitalize and protect empaths. They can be carried in the pocket, or in a purse. Furthermore, they can be used as jewelry. You can adorn yourself with them in the form of rings, pendants, and earrings. Be mindful that what works for another empath who have similar issues may not necessarily work for you. Here are some of the popular gemstones.

Rose quartz

If you have been hurt emotionally whether in childhood or as an adult, this gemstone helps. It is like having unconditional love wrapped pretty in a gemstone. When dealing with negative people and situations keep rose quartz close.

Amethyst

This gemstone magnetizes positive energy and repels negative vibrations. It is used for protection. It also improves your intuition.

Black Tourmaline

If you are constantly around narcissists and energy leeches, black tourmaline shields and protects you. If you are a healer and always withdrawing negativity from people, protect yourself by using it.

Blue Topaz

It can be used for mental clarity and to aid with communicating what you want.

Hermatite

This is a strong grounding gemstone. It has powerful effects when you wear it while barefooted. It helps you to feel stronger and more centered.

Jade

Jade is used to harmonize the energy between partners. It calms the nerves and reduces fear.

Turquoise

This gemstone is known for its power and protective qualities. Negative energy is repelled with this gemstone.

Malachite

When you have emotional obstacles and you're dealing with worrying and a demanding state of affairs, use malachite.

Lapis Lazuli

It enhances the way you think and gives clarity. It is also a protective gemstone and reflects the negative energy back to the source. If you are an introvert, it aids you in expressing yourself.

Red Jasper

This stone has a powerful connection to the earth and is used in grounding. It gives stability and greater insight. It gives protection and is used when someone has to travel at night. It also gives confidence.

Citrine

This gemstone is also called Citron, Citrina, Merchant Stone and Success Stone. It gives energy, success, prosperity, and confidence. It is used for meditation purposes and awareness.

Moonstone

Moonstone is used for inner strength and is an emotion stabilizer. It gives spiritual insights and is used when an empath is starting afresh and anew. It represents new beginnings.

Yellow Sapphire

It attracts wealth and abundance. It calms and stimulates the mind and helps you to concentrate on your goals.

Onyx

Onyx is a protective gemstone. It repels negative energy and gives harmony in relationships.

Smoky Quartz

It balances the environment and is great for grounding. It dispels fear and negativity. If you are depressed, this stone will also improve your mood. It also alleviates headaches.

Zodiac signs

If you are someone who pays attention to the zodiac signs here are some of the gemstones that are compatible with your sign as well as being an aid as an empath. Note that there are several stones that can be worn.

Capricorn

Onyx and Smoky Quartz are the stones for individuals who are Capricorns. Capricorns are hardworking and responsible, many times missing out on the excitement that life offers. Onyx helps them to achieve their goals and brings harmony to them.

Smoky Quartz will help empaths from caving or collapsing from all the responsibilities. It eases the pressures and dispels negative vibrations.

Pisces

Amethyst represents protection and strength to those born under this sign. They will be courageous when the need arises. It gives them the resourcefulness to express themselves.

Aquarius

The water carrier is the symbol for this sign. Turquoise stabilizes mood swings and neutralizes the emotions.

Other gemstones that can be used are Malachite and Jade. If individuals have dreams and can't seem to decipher their meaning, Malachite brings matters to a higher consciousness. You will also have courage and more self-esteem. Jade has a calming effect and balances individuals who are often restless and in search for a different experience.

Aries

Red Jasper assists with being more creative when communicating. It also gives deeper understanding. Another stone that can be used is Hematite which helps with personal growth and gives strength.

Taurus

Individuals born under this sign are persistent. Lapis lazuli is great for those who need a lot of patience. It also helps with communication. Another stone that can be used is Rose Quartz.

Cancer

Individuals born under this sign are gentle, caring, intuitive, and highly imaginative. Moonstone is great for emotional well-being and help with clairvoyance and intuition.

Gemini

The sign has the twin symbol. They have a lot of energy, expressive and can change their minds constantly.

Citrine helps with prosperity and gives energy. As the symbol is that of duality, individuals are quick to make decisions and change in an instant. This gemstone will bring a deeper awareness to help them in decision making.

Leo

Leos have a very strong personality and are very expressive. Citrine is associated with positive energy, happiness, and success.

Onyx helps Leos to have more self-control and helps them not to spend all of their time and energy on unproductive things.

Virgo

Yellow Sapphire and Red Jasper are the stones to use for individuals born under this sign.

Yellow sapphire is great for those who are reluctant to express how they feel. It also is great for deeper insight. Red Jasper gives harmony and fortifies strength.

Libra

Smoky Quartz helps with healing and wounds that have been hidden and forgotten. It gives the empath courage. It should be placed close to the entrance of your personal environment if you to keep it at home. Moonstone is also another gemstone used by individuals born under this zodiac sign.

Scorpio

This is one of the highly emotional signs for they can be very expressive with a biting tongue.

They are also focused. Onyx is good for reducing irritation and anger. Moonstone is also another gemstone that can be used by Scorpions.

Sagittarius

Turquoise, Amethyst and Lapis lazuli can be used for those born under this sign. Turquoise helps with attaining goals. Amethyst is great for protection and diminishes fear and stress. Lapis lazuli is also great for protection and gives better clarity. Blue Topaz also helps with mental clarity.

Chapter 9: Self Care and Feng Shui

Self-Care Tips

Empaths need to pay lots of attention to self-care. Here are some habits that you should incorporate in your routine

Get enough sleep

Ensure that you obtain the required hours of sleep necessary for the restorative process. Some individuals can thrive on five or six hours of sleep others may need seven to eight hours. It's a personal choice. However, functioning on two hours or three hours of sleep daily especially when you are only now conscious that you are an empath is not sufficient rest. Empaths need to be alert.

Be aware of the effect if you sleep with crystals or gemstones

Crystals and gemstones have their own vibration. If you keep them close while sleeping, they may alter your frequency. If you notice this, and you are not sleeping well, keep them away from you while sleeping.

On the other hand, some empaths have them close while sleeping. It is a preference but if you are just becoming more enlightened about who you are, be aware that they can affect your frequency.

Monitor your exposure to media and the news

It's necessary to know what is happening in your state and country and the rest of the world. It doesn't mean though, that you should be affixed to the news channel at the top of every hour and the media platforms. This will cause you to be very overwhelmed.

Balance your mood by viewing movies and reading articles that will make you feel at peace and make you happy.

De-clutter

Things have energy. You may feel an attachment to something but you must know when it is time to let go of certain things. Do not hold on to things out of obligation or you may feel guilt-ridden about disposing them.

Tips for de-cluttering

• Be conscious of what is entering your home. If you are simply removing stuff, only to fill the space again with unnecessary stuff, then the exercise is futile. Be mindful of what you replace the empty space with.

- Take your time. Remember it's a process. There is no need to feel harassed or be overwhelmed. Take it one step at a time or start with the easy bits first.
- Go through and decide what you will donate, throw away and sell.

Avoid drama

As you learn from your experiences you will know that certain friends and family members drain your energy more than others. You will have to know when to shorten your conversations or prevent them from unburdening to you by having boundaries.

If you're feeling very tired, decipher when the energy is yours or when it's someone else's energy.

Say NO more often

By nature, empaths want to help and will put themselves last. However, you have to know when to dive in and help, when to send positive energy to guide others on their journey and when to simply wish them well while focusing on yourself. Saying 'no' doesn't make you a bad person. When you say 'no' you shouldn't feel guilty. Saying 'no' is an opportunity for you to care for yourself better.

Spend time outdoors

Take leisure walks. You don't have to spend an hour or two hours outdoors. Even fifteen minutes can do wonders. If your environment is safe and clean, walk barefoot on the grass. Infuse joy and laughter in your life

Pay attention to your schedule

Be mindful of the times when you are feeling overwhelmed and how your schedule impacts your energy. For example, if you noticed that when you have a busy schedule that your energy is low, then in future you will need to schedule appointments with sufficient time frame to balance your energy. If you are unable to do so, then surround yourself with light. Keep gemstones that will balance your mood, close to you.

Meditate

Engage in meditation to eradicate negative energy.

Feng shui

Feng shui is an art form that originated in China. It teaches how to harmonize energy in an environment. Feng when translated means wind and shui, is water. Your space should reflect who you are and who you aspire to be.

What is it that you wish to change? Do you constantly feel burdened and stressed out? If you are, it is time to change your living space. It doesn't mean that your problems will all go away. However, it will give you the space to breathe, think and focus on what you need to do to find solutions to your problems. The list is not exhaustive but the objective is for you to have more peace.

Have more light

Draw the curtains and open the blinds to let the sunlight in. Light dispels darkness. If you feel heaviness in your environment, let the light in. Depending on the season, if possible, step outside and let the sunlight warn your face and body.

If you have your furniture arranged so that it blocks the windows, rearranged them.

Purify your environment

Use incense, crystals, and essential oils to purify your space and lift your mood. We have already discussed this in previous chapters.

Clean your environment

Empaths do not need to see dust to know that a place needs cleaning. They can feel the muck. When feeling low on energy and nothing seems to work, try cleaning your environment. It will make you feel lighter and better in spirit.

Use plants

Perhaps you have plants in your home but didn't have such a deep understanding of their energy as you do now. Having plants in your surroundings is like having Mother Nature in your home. Plants clean the air and gives you a radiant energy.

Use color

If certain areas in your space make you feel dull and numb, incorporate colors. Everyone has a particular color or colors he or she prefers. However, some colors have a specific feeling. You know that red, orange, and yellow give warmth and energy. Blue, green and turquoise produce a relaxing and cool atmosphere. Mix and blend with other colors until you find the colors that give you the right energy.

Ornaments

Some empaths are drawn to certain ornaments. Perhaps it may be elephants or a dancing ballerina or turtles. Whatever it may be, once they calm your spirit and bring you peace, consider arranging them in certain areas in your environment.

Conclusion

Thank you for making it through to the end of *Empath: Empowering empaths, healing, sensitive emotions, energy & relationships*. I do hope it was informative and able to provide you with the tools you need to achieve your goals.

If you are someone who didn't know before that you're an empath you now understand why people are drawn to you. You are a great listener. People feel better after being around you. They are so comfortable around you that they are always clinging to you. Your phone rings very often when someone has a problem. Nothing is wrong with listening and helping but you have to be vigilant not to be an emotional garbage bin.

You are armed with a wealth of knowledge on how to ground and shield. Sometimes you also have to know when ignoring and walking away is best. Some people do not want to develop and heal. They like the attention so make sure when you help you have set your boundaries and know when enough is enough.

On the flipside, some empaths appear cold and standoffish. It is not that they are cold but they do not know how to balance and find harmony with who they are and what other people expect of them. If you fall in this category, do not shut everyone out. Life is for living. In our opening chapters I explored various ways on how you can establish boundaries. You can say 'no' politely and with a smile.

You can also consider getting a pet if you don't have any, to lift your spirit. Do not live life depressed and lonely. Take time to heal, and live life with purpose.

The next step is to embrace who you are. You are not weird and you are not paranoid. You are unique and have a big heart filled with love. You were born this way and the sooner you come to terms with it, the more you will enjoy the wonderful things that life has to offer. Respect who you are and implement ways to invite more positive energy in your life. You absolutely deserve it!

EMOTIONAL HEALING

Coping With Emotional & Psychological Trauma

MELISSA A. HOLLOWAY

Emotional Healing

Coping with Emotional and Psychological Trauma

By Melissa Anna Holloway

Introduction

Thank you for purchasing your own personal copy of *Emotional Healing: Coping with Emotional and Psychological Trauma.*

The following chapters will discuss some of the tragedies we unfortunately are susceptible to in life, and why they wreak so much havoc on us as human beings. But the main portion of this book is to help those discover ways that they can rise from the ashes that life has left them with, and make the best of them.

You will discover how important emotional healing is in terms of emotional and psychological trauma, and the various ways that one has to choose from in healing themselves. Each and every one of us is different, both inside and out. It is crucial that we dig deep within ourselves to provide the best care we can. It is true what they say: Only YOU are in charge of your ultimate happiness in life. Isn't it time you take back the reigns and become in control once again?

The chapters of this book will cover what emotional healing is itself, as well as the various ways one can try and learn from when it comes to self-healing. You do not necessarily need a doctor, therapist or psychiatrist to assist you in your journey of healing. In fact, one feels much more powerful when they can get back to feeling themselves BY themselves. It's kind of a win-win.

While there are lots of varieties of books regarding information about emotional healing, this book in specific covers information that is not only based upon resources from the World Wide Web or from other books, but also from personal experience. Every effort was made to ensure that this book is packed with vital information to help you in your emotional healing journey. Good luck!

Emotional Healing: How Did We Get This Wrecked?

Ah, the journey of life. It is exciting, scary, ridiculous, confusing and worth it all at once. But there are times that we all go through some type of emotional distress, whether it be mere sadness, rapid anxiety, addictions to outside influences, obsessions with things or people, compulsions we have a hard time controlling, behaviors that are self-sabotaging, physical injuries, anger, and bleak moods, among the hundreds of other things we go through, think and/or feel.

It is important to learn ways to cope when it comes to hard times, no matter the time frame. Something psychologically downgrading can happen in a matter of mere moments and leave you scarred for the rest of your life. Some people seek out help from other individuals who are professionals at understanding the human mind, but others wish to find help within themselves. Having the knowledge to help yourself is not an easy feat. It may be easy to read pages upon pages of books and self-help websites that provide information, but it is much harder to put those words into actions.

The world is a much different place now than it was just a decade or two ago. Technology has advanced so rapidly that some of us are overwhelmed with it all, especially the consequences that we receive, whether from our own actions or that of another being who acted upon a current mood. Human beings are not the robots that we seem to want to create so badly these days. We are emotionally driven individuals with a lack of having the knack to help ourselves in times of need and/or trouble.

The worst thing about the constant rise of this distress is the fact that there is no one age group or certain targeted individuals that are more likely to go through it. It is happening clear from late grade school levels all the ways into senior living years. Students have much more stress with perpetual levels of testing and pressure to be better. Employees live their hard earned careers always fighting to make their way up the ladder with not much reward. Older individuals are continuously having their wages and retirement that they worked their entire lives for whisked away. Etc, etc, etc.

It is a dog eat dog world out there with a lot of room to make mistakes that can cause even more friction in our personal lives. With the constant pressure to be better than the next, our society has taught us maybe how to be more proficient in terms of getting things done at school or work, but many of us have forgotten the person that is truly important: OURSELVES. If we do not take care of our emotional health, detrimental things can occur. Below are some signs that you may be experiencing emotional distress. Some of the symptoms may surprise you.

Signs and Symptoms of Emotional Distress

Disturbances or changes in sleep

- Sleeping more or less than the usual
- Troubles falling and staying asleep
- Waking up after a couple hours of sleep and not being able to get back into a slumber

Constant reoccurring issues when it comes to sleeping habits, meaning more than once or twice a week, may be a sign of a psychological issue, most likely depression and/or anxiety.

Fluctuations in Weight

- Significant loss or weight gain
- Perpetual thinking about food and eating

If your mind is continuously preoccupied by the idea of food, your weight and the way you see yourself (body image) then you may have a type of eating disorder that is taking away your energy from other significant portions of your life.

Unidentified Changes

Even if you are one that works out on a regular basis and have seen a doctor regarding physical complaints, there may be a deeper reason to why your body is hurting with no estranged ailment. It may be signaling you that you are distressed. These could be chronic pains, constipation, diarrhea, stomach upsets, headaches, etc.

Difficulty in Controlling Temper

If you are emotionally stable when you are by yourself but easily angered or annoyed when it comes to being around your co-workers, friends, children or spouse, than this may be a major sign of an overload of stress that can cause extreme harm to you inside and out. It is also very unhealthy for those around you that have to put up with you when acting upon these distress signals. This is a sign that one cannot properly manage their feelings and should possibly see a psychologist, or that or the like.

Obsessive Behavior(s)

- Always on a mission to wash hands no matter the current location
- Worry about things that might happen
- Have rituals such as touching certain items that take up a lot of your time

If you have any of the above or similar symptoms controlling your life, there may be more than just anxiety ruling over you.

Repetitive thoughts or actions that harbor worry are paired with anxiety. If your mind becomes totally obsessed with these obsessions, your life can be taken completely over by anxiety and emotional distress.

Constant Tiredness and/or Lack of Energy

If you are constantly feeling too tired to enjoy that things that give you happiness, this is a major sign of distress. If the body is overloaded by emotional distress, it can physically shut down, which can cause this feeling of constant fatigue.

Issues with Memory

There are quite a few factors that can essentially play into troubles regarding one's memory, like hormonal changes and lack of sleep, for example. But stress is another major factor, no matter if it's a backlash of some kind of traumatic event or otherwise. Anxiety and depression could be the cause for this symptom. Forgetfulness is also a mechanism of the mind, which protects us from traumatic thoughts from certain events.

Avoiding Being Social

- Avoid texts and calls from friends that you once enjoyed hanging out with on a regular basis
- Okay at work then would rather lay in bed and sleep than do anything else when you return home
- Turning down invites from others because you would much rather stay home

The above are all warning signs that your emotions are taking more of a toll on you than you may like to admit. Major changes in behaviors regarding your social life can be a red flag that you are overloaded with stress. Or you may have an undiagnosed fear or phobia that is keeping you locked up in your house without any chains.

Lack of Sex Drive

- Does sex not pleasure you like it once did
- In love with your sexual partner but have no interest in making love

If nothing seems to be wrong when you get a regular checkup with your doctor, chances are that depression, anxiety and/or emotional distress may be the cause for your lack of interest in sexual activity. The distress might be coming right from your relationship, but chances are it is stress from an entirely different part of your life, wreaking havoc on other precious areas.

Mood Swings or Unexplained Behavior(s)

You may not notice it, but if you are having regular bouts of mood swings or other behaviors that are not normally like you, your friends, family and those closest to you are sure to take notice. It is crucial to listen to those that you surround your life with as well, not just your own voice trying to convince you that things are normal as usual. If there are more and more individuals commenting on your actions, then it might be time to take a step back and take action to correct it.

As mentioned before, all of us are different in our own unique ways, both inside and out. But to be the best we can be on the outside, we must treasure and fuel our insides with positivity and take care of our emotional and mental state of minds. Our brains are the conductor for how we act and observe the world, yet at most times, it is the part of our body that is the most taken for granted. The rest of this book contains chapters to help alleviate distress symptoms through ways other than speaking to a health care provider or consuming various kinds of prescriptions or narcotics.

Think of your life as driving on a beautiful highway. If you do not keep the windshield clean, you are missing out on all the wonder and opportunities that surround you and are anxiously awaiting your arrival. Isn't it about time you gained control of your emotional state of mind?

How to Find and Learn to Love Yourself Again after Trauma

Even during durations of tough times, many of us tend to at least try our best to have the positive mindset that things will get better with time. But what we forget is that we need to take the time to look within ourselves, give our inner beings a bit of credit and learn how to truly self-love and appreciate ourselves for who we are. Honestly, we all need to give ourselves a pat on the back more often. Life is not an easy feat and there is always something around the corner, ready to bite us in the butt at the most inconvenient of times.

There are several different reasons as to why people grow up feeling a bit crumby about themselves from the start and why learning to love oneself as well as other can be rather difficult:

- They were not loved or well taken care of by parents or guardians
- They were not shown love in unconditional ways, but rather in destructive manners
- They were only loved unconditionally when the parents or guardians approved of their decisions and choice
- They were loved but did not have anyone protecting them from harm's way

Many of us have at some point or another have been treated wrongly by someone in our life, whether it be significant others, family members, friends, etc. No one is guarded from the world of hurt there is out there. As a result from the maiming of other people, we see ourselves as unlovable beings, which fuel those long hate speeches some have in the mirror every morning before heading out into the vast world. But what we do not realize is the fact that we are keeping our souls trapped within a vicious traumatic cycle. We have to be able to give to ourselves what we were not adequately provided growing up or during young adulthood. The big pictured goal is to get past issues from your past so that you can focus more on your future and better your state a mind to a more positive note.

Despite the Nicholas Spark's novels and cliché love and romance movies, loving yourself IS indeed the ultimate act of love and kindness. You cannot properly extend love to others if you have nothing to give from. Until you love yourself for who you are and who you are becoming, there will always be a void that you so desperately attempt to fill by letting people into your life that do not actually deserve your love. This will lead to disappointment and even more heart break if you do not put an end to this cycle NOW. Easier said than done, of course.

Even for those that have been to hell and back thanks to their abusive upbringings, learning how to love all parts of who you are is crucial. You can try your damnest to go back and claw at those that should have loved you better from your past, but those individuals are not going to fill that void that they were the creators of. Loving yourself is the only way to life yourself up high enough to reach the ladder to the podium of happiness.

Loving yourself, just like having that warm, fuzzy feeling of loving anything or anyone else, is not a choice, but rather a domino effect of actions based upon the new-found decision to take pride in your life and love truly love yourself. Even before you give yourself a kiss on the cheek or a pat on the back, you need to start taking actions, even if you feel more hate towards yourself than love at first. Quite literally you have to "fake it before you make it" in this instance. Loving yourself takes time and dedication to go out of your way to resolve negative actions and create more positive ones from them. Loving yourself also means learning to love others for who THEY are on the inside, leaving outside appearances to the birds. Looks are almost always deceiving.

The rest of this chapter is filled with ideas to act upon in the terms of loving yourself and who you are. I hope you enjoy and find some that will work for you! Sometimes, no matter how hard headed or resilient we are to change, it is better to just out your best foot forward and take that leap! You may be very surprised at the ways you can mold yourself into a better individual, inside and out!

Learning to Love Yourself: Ideas for Course of Action

Stop the negative self-talk and fill that void with the bright light of positive facts. Put more focus onto the things that are great about you and the things that you could improve as that, things to improve over time! And if you are one of those that are in a deep negative hole, you may find that seeking the assistance of those that now you the best to be crucial. The simpler the ideas, the better. It is of your best interest to begin small and work your way up to bigger aspects about your being.

Learn to tell yourself positive affirmations, no matter how much you believe them or not. It is not about accepting the positive things you tell yourself during the course of your day; it is about identifying the core of the hate that impedes you from being positive. If you constantly tell yourself that you are unable to be loved, then make the effort to change around the wording to a positive manner. Think to yourself that you are indeed able to be loved, no matter the circumstances or how others view you as.

Learn how to comfort yourself, whether spending time alone or with others. Create your own list of positive behaviors that can be utilized to reduce stress or to even just pamper yourself.

Keep that list in a place where you will see it often, especially during daily routines. Examples could be going on a walk, wearing your favorite set of clothes, drinking a cup of your favorite tea, etc. You list will vary depending on your personality, as well as will become better with time as you continue to work on yourselves.

Keep a list of things that you like about yourself and change this list up on a daily basis. This is especially important on those long, tough days where all you want to do is back into your negative hole.

Applaud yourself and your accomplishments, no matter how big or small they are. Add it to your list of daily positivity that is described above.

Learn how to love your body, especially the imperfections. Instead of viewing your bodies "inadequacies" as such, view them as parts of your physical being that makes you unique! Make sure to treat your body as a temple, well, because it is! Without our bodies what other vessel would our souls have to walk this amazing planet we reside on? Exercise regularly. Catch enough zzz's. Fuel your body in healthy ways, etc.

Center your attention around compassion for yourself by turning your love for others back around on yourself, reflecting and basking in that warm glow!

Invest in yourself by spending at least 15-30 minutes per day either in the morning or evening before bed by listening to your favorite music, watching positive material that inspires you on television, reading a novel that fulfills you, anything that comforts you and that assists you in understanding you at the most rawest core.

Find both the omission and validity within your own inner and outer circles. Your inner circle of individuals in your life may not say the nicest things about you, bringing you down to server their own selfish purposes, which can cause you more self-harm than good. So, what is an exception regarding this? Good question. First and foremost, it is crucial to mold your thoughts in a positive manner to be able to find the truth while not getting yourself down. For example, if someone informs you that you are not doing very well in school, ask yourself the right questions and seek the answers that either validates their feelings or either dismisses them. Most times, you are probably doing a heck of a lot better job than you believe and those individuals are just jealous of your success and want to taint your success.

Learn to escape by utilizing your favorite ways of winding down. This could be a long hot bubble bath, or reading a good book to get away from the current world. Ensure that you make about half an hour of time daily to reward your body for making it through the turmoil of the present day.

Appreciate yourself in little ways every single day. This helps in creating a more balanced idea of positive self-preservation. Write in a journal or keep a notepad on your smart phone or computer. What are at least three things you acknowledge about yourself in a positive manner? It could be anything, from good listener or doing your hobby very well. Things you appreciate about yourself could be as small as conducting constant and everyday oral hygiene.

Always learn to take at a step towards positivity, even if they are baby steps. If you feel like you lived through a mediocre type of day, ensure that you take a step toward a brighter state of mind at some point during the course of the 24 hours we have each and every day. Find things that give you a sense of hope or bring a type of optimism to your mind. Maybe it is time to attempt a new hobby, seek ways that you can go further in your career. Setup a dinner date with a friend, or maybe even research a possible trip you wish to take in the future.

Follow the Golden Rule. Yup, Mom was right. Treating people with a kinder hand or the way you wish you were treated goes way farther than any dollar can buy. Making a conscious effort to act more gracious towards others will eventually lead to being nicer to yourself as well. It can be anything, even random acts of kindness towards strangers. Don't see these acts as something to be paid back. Just be on a constant move to pay if forward and good karma will greet you with open arms. Listening to someone vent, helping someone reach something on a grocery store shelf, encouraging friends or family when they need a helping hand or even just letting someone into your lane while driving all are classified as these random acts.

Learn how to be your own best friend. If you constantly are on a path to self-destruct, it will wear away at you and erode your self-worthiness. Learn how to ask yourself about things as if you are asking friends or family for help in certain situations. Talk to yourself like your loved ones would. Always remember to learn from your mistakes and how to take ample opportunities from your missteps. We are all human beings and need to learn that we are allowed to make mistakes.

When it comes down to it, **learn to embrace a good laughing session**. Utilizing 5-10 minutes per day for pure, unadulterated laughter is one of the best methods to alleviate stress. If it takes going into your vault of funny Facebook videos to get the job done, by all means! Laughter is one of the best medicines and the best perk is that it is totally free and you should feel free to rival in laughs as often as you like. Laughter can be a useful and effective way to recharge energy and positivity to release all that tension that has built up inside of you.

Always keep the future in mind and **remember it is never too late for change**. It is easy to get stuck in the humdrum of everyday chaotic life. It sometimes may seem that life is constantly kicking you to the curb, leaving you only wondering where in the world you went wrong. But trust me, you didn't! Of course, there may have been another decision that could have worked out better, but you made certain choices for the right reasons at the time. Instead of dwelling on past choices or regrets, look ahead toward the future. In the present you can shape what your future looks like. Make goals and makes lists as to steps to obtain those goals.

Remind yourself that it's smart to be kind to yourself, always. After reading through these many reasons as to why it is vital to learn the ways to be kinder to your inner being, it will become easier reminding yourself to be in a more positive state of mind. The more you practice this, the easier it is to instill positive practices. As you have read, there are a plethora of benefits in living more positively and it helps you build your self-esteem and build up your inner happiness, which assists in instilling better, more positively fueled relationships within your life. If anything, try your best every single day to make a bright domino effect happen around you. The world will eventually reward you graciously ten-fold!

Coping with Exercise

We all know that an inevitable part of life is the heavy downpours of stress. In fact, 7 out of 10 adults in America tell researchers that they are anxious, stressed and/or depressed and that it impacts their personal lives on a regular basis. Stress is impossible to 100% eliminate but there are ways that it can be successfully managed. This chapter is filled with the easiest and most prominent way of coping with stress as well as distress: means of physical activity.

Exercise not only assists us in feeling ultimately better about ourselves when it comes to our mental health, but the physical aspects of our body thank us for utilizing them to the best of their ability as well. Our doctors encourage us constantly about getting outdoors, breathing in some fresh air and working out stressed muscles. Exercise is the key to the fitness of our mental state of mind. Many varieties have shown that adding physical activities to your daily lifestyle can help reduce tiredness, improve the amount of concentration and improve the overall function of our cognitive abilities. Exercise is kind of seen like a battery backup, when life has taken away a portion of your energy, exercise gives you a boost to be able to concentrate and continue on your tough treks!

Many of us do not realize that stress and/or distress quite literally burns up nerve connections in our brain, which leaves the remainder of our bodies feeling the impact in negative ways. So, if your body feels better, the brain feels the positive countenances that our body endures. Exercise is a natural painkiller, with the great side effect of saving your kidneys and liver from so much over-usage. It produces loads of endorphins, which reduces stress almost immediately. And it doesn't stop there. If you add exercise in everyday, you will be able to sleep better and think more clearly as well.

So, why don't more of us take the time to take better care of our bodies and exercise? Because we assume we do not have time, or avoid it because we are so worn out from the day's activities. It is much easier said than done to incorporate something that we would otherwise not do. But why pop pills to reduce tension, stabilize our moods, help our sleep cycles and help us see ourselves in a more positive manner when we can simply add moving around more? Exactly! Just five short minutes of aerobic activity can help get those anti-anxiety fluids running and working their magic.

It has been shown many times that exercise alone, without the need for medications helps reduce some of the worst symptoms of depression and anxiety. The effects of it last much longer than any narcotics on the market as well. Energetic sessions of physical activity can reduce symptoms for quite a few hours, so imagine what incorporating regular exercise into your everyday routine could do for you!

Ways that Exercise Reduces Stress

Looking into a deeper aspect of exercise, it **helps your body practice and become used to how to deal with emotional stress** as well. When your body is in a state of distress, its inner systems, such as nervous, muscular, cardiovascular etc, have a job to act simultaneously to manage stress effectively. Physical activity helps our bodies exercise and learn to utilize those systems in an appropriate manner. For example, when you go for a simple walk or possibly a walk, you are kick starting your muscular systems, as well as the respiratory and cardiovascular ones too. They determine how to communicate with each other. This means when stress occurrences that induce stress hormones to act up, our bodies know how to counteract them in a better manner! Our bodies are beyond awesome!

We have already talked about the benefits of a **raised level of endorphins** and exercise is the main way to hype those levels up to fuel us into feeling great! Endorphins are a ways more natural form of the typical pharmaceutical pain killer and can give us a certain 'high' that narcotic provide us, but makes our organs much happier. Long extents of time that we spend conducting ourselves in high intensity activities increase the discharge of this feel good hormone. This obviously means that there will be a natural rising of your spirit, leaving you less susceptible to falling into a depressed slump.

While exercise raises endorphin levels, it **lowers the levels of the hormones that go into our innate response of "fight or flight."** Thanks to all the stress we are under, even though we may not always be in immediate danger, stress induces these hormones to be raised in our bodies, which is why we feel even more antsy than the usual. Going on a walk, jog or run helps and it is utilizing those raised negative hormones in a good way rather than having them just reside in our bodies.

Exercising on a regular basis helps our bodies get into a natural rhythm and balances out our equilibrium. This especially goes for cycling, running and/or lifting. Measured flows of action help our bodies relax. This is why runners go out to "clear their head." Yes, it is actually a thing!

Even though exercising is a great solo activity to engage in, two or more is better than one in this case! Going to an exercise class or joining a workout group allows you to interact with other people like you, who may be going through the same daily stresses and trying to rid them in the same manner. Interaction is also a great way to dispense al that negative energy out of your body.

Exercise helps us handle stress, which **enables us to receive more adequate sleep**. Raised stress levels assists with our minds not being able to shut off when our heads hit the pillow and lack of sleep fuels up those negative hormones during the day rather than the other way around. Engaging in physical activity also allows us to feel more tired, allowing us to fall asleep quicker when bedtime comes as well.

Many people feel very stressed out when their lives are not organized or planned out in a certain way. A chaotic life is like gasoline for stress to flare up. It is important to set weekly goals and remain on a schedule, at least in some sort or another. This doesn't mean to become so busy that you always stick to a schedule and never anything else. Life is not meant to be lived that way. Goals help us to get high enough to reach our achievements. If we pride ourselves to incorporating an exercise plan into our lives, **it can initiate us to become more organized in all aspects of our everyday lives**.

If you are able to walk on your own two feet without the assistance of human-made equipment, you should feel super lucky to be able to exercise at all. So, if you are feeling gloomy, instead of popping a prescribed pill or drinking a tall glass of wine (not that drinking is off the table), maybe you should put on your running shoes and go for a walk around the block or two. Work your way up, but do not exercise too much at once. Then you will be discouraged to do so on a more regular basis. Exercise is a type of cure all. Relieving stress and other bodily ailments.

Coping with Meditation and Prayer

You have learned how exercise can help melt away the stress of the every day. What if you could take with you another type of stress relief with you, absolutely anywhere without having to leave your home? It is possible! This chapter is going to go into some detail about the methods of meditation and the action of daily prayer can help keep your mind at ease!

Meditation to Relieve Stress

Meditation is known to bring those that act upon it to bring them inner peace, no matter the negativity that had washed over them during the day. It is an easy way to practice stress relief wherever you are too! It may take one awhile to master the ways of meditating, but once you become accustomed to it and practice it often, even just a couple minutes a day could improve your state of mind. You could even practice meditation while you are exercising!

Meditation has been a stress relief practice for hundreds of thousands of years and was actually used to grasp an understanding of mystical forces. But for the most part, it is utilized as a method of stress reduction. It is considered a body and mind interdependent type of medication, giving one a state of relaxation quite unlike anything else. During the course of meditating, you are supposed to focus on eliminating your many negative thoughts that might be overwhelming you. Meditation is used more so as an enhancement of your well-being, emotionally and physically. It is utilized as a tool for stress management, especially as a balancer in your life. In fact, there is research to back up the fact that meditation can reverse the effects of every day stress.

Benefits of Meditation

Meditation provides our bodies with a sense of calmness, slowing down our heart rate and allowing us to take in the air around us at a slower pace. Our blood pressures become stable and we begin to practice the art of utilizing the oxygen we take in more effectively, causing us to sweat less as well. The benefits of meditation, just like exercise, do not abruptly stop when you are finished with a session. Its methods allow one to live more calmly throughout the course of a typical day, which can drastically improve various medical conditions that one may already have or has a risk of getting. Within the body, this slows down the process of aging and even bumps up our immune functions! And your state of mind is a heck of a lot clearer, which can lead to better decision making skills, which will hopefully put you on a path to a life full of less regret in the future.

And the benefits of meditation do not stop on the physical aspect of things either. It is a superb practice when it comes to aiding our emotional well-being too!

- Reduction of negative emotions and/or thoughts
- Ability to remain and truly focus on the present
- Raises our levels of self-awareness
- Helps us build strong skill sets to deal and manage present and future stress
- Allows us room to gain perspectives we would have otherwise not seen

Different Types of Meditation

Meditation, in a sense, is actually well known as a place we are in within our mind, a relaxed state, if you will. There is a variety of types of relaxation tips and techniques when it comes to meditation methods, it is important to know the vital components of each one. But all boil down to having the same initial goals in reaching a type of inner peace within ourselves.

- **Yoga** – Yoga is a practice in which one acts within a series of particular postures and using breathing exercises. Yoga is a type of mediation that advocates us to become more flexible beings and remain in a calm state of mind while doing so. The series of poses allow those to practice balance through concentration, which teaches those to leave their worries at the door for a bit and think more in the moment, to be attached directly to your mind, rather than the thoughts that trouble you.

- **Transcendental** – This method is a natural approach in which one repeats an assigned a personal melody, whether it be a phrase, sound or particular word, in a certain manner. Doing this allows your body to get into a state of mind that promotes relaxation and to get your mind into a state of inner peace without the need of too much concentration.

- **Tai chi** – This method is a way into Chinese martial arts. It allows one to act in a series of movements in a slow and graceful way all the while practicing deep breathing techniques.

- **Qi gong** – This method is a small part of Chinese medicine that is a combo of breathing exercises, physical movement, relaxation and meditation.

- **Mindfulness meditation** – Just like its namesake, this method of meditation is all about being mindful of oneself, or in other words an upper level of self-awareness and wanting to live within the present moment.

- **Mantra meditation** – This method requires us to repeat a calming type of word or phrase to prevent thoughts that would otherwise distract us.

- **Guided meditation** – This method is also known to some as visualization, which utilizes the form of mentally produced images or occurrences you have experienced that are relaxed. This form of meditation is majorly used during therapy sessions, with clients using their five senses and usually requires a teacher or therapist to lead one into this state of mind.

Essentials of Meditation

Each of the different types of meditation requires different aspects to assist in the course of particular meditations. It all depends on the guidance in which you seek to receive from your meditation methods.

- **Focused attention** – The ability to focus all your attention to one general aspect is a crucial part of meditation. This gives your mind the freedom it deserves, eliminating stress, worry and other distractions.

- **Comfortable position(s)** – It is important to remain comfortable when you are performing any kind of meditation. This is vital when it comes to getting the absolute most out of these sessions.

- **Quiet space** – Especially if you are a beginner when it comes to the ways of meditation, a quiet setting is crucial, otherwise those distractions will increase and shut down you wanting to become less stressed. This means no television watching, cell phone usage or listening to the radio. As you become more skilled in your meditation, you can perform them in situations such as traffic jams or stressful meetings at work.

- **Relaxed breathing** – This portion of meditation is perhaps the most important aspect. This involves one who performs deep and even breathing, utilizing the lungs and diaphragm muscles. The reason it is so important because the usage of these muscles decreases the use of chest, shoulder and neck muscles, where many of us tend to carry the most stress in our bodies.

Ways to Practice Meditation in Everyday Situation

Many people try and then stop trying forms of meditation because the thought of doing it the "correct" way adds another level of stress on top of everything else. That is quite the opposite of what those that conduct themselves in meditating ways should do. This is why beginners start out in classes and them practice on their own over time. Everyone is a little different and chooses to use the ways of meditation. Some incorporate it into their daily routines and others use it as stress builds within them. The following are some great ways to practice and utilize meditation on their own time.

Center your attention on gratitude and love – This method of meditation requires one to focus all their attention on a certain being or thing, weaving into those things love and compassion, with a pinch of good ol' gratitude into your thoughts. Either close your eyes and use your imagination or peer right at the subject itself.

Read and Emulate – There are many individuals that get quite a bit of positivity from the reading of poems and other such texts, ensuring to take time to reflect on what the text really means. Listening to relaxing music or spoken words can also be relaxing and/or inspiring. Recording these mental reflections on paper is also a great way to peer over them later and talk about them with those close to you that may also benefit from them.

Walk and Meditate – Combining a bit of easy exercise with meditating is quite the pair. It is both healthy for anyone doing it as it is efficient, especially in a time crunch. Slow down your pace and focus on each movement that your legs perform. Do not worry about the destination in which you are going towards. Just on the movements of your legs and feet, repeating words and actions.

Scan your body – With this method, one must hone in on each part of their body, which also includes the sensations in which they feel too. Combine this with deep breathing exercises, all the while imagining that you are breathing in and out the feeling of heat to those areas.

Prayer to Relieve Stress

The act of prayer is known to greatly help in many aspects of our lives, but did you know that it is quite the tool to help manage and/or reduce stress? But which prayers are the most worthwhile when it comes to lessening our daily worries? You are in luck! The following are the best to recite when you need a boost of hope in a time of need and to calm the soul. These Psalms are ones that they recited back thousands of years ago when people needed a bit of inspiration to fight going forward.

Many people are pretty familiar with the Serenity Prayer and not just because it is the most famous and inspiring prayer in Christianity, but because it eases peace of mind. And if you are not, it may be one you want to print out and get preoccupied with.

The Serenity Prayer

"God grant me the serenity to accept the things I cannot change; courage to change the things I can; and wisdom to know the difference. Living one day at a time; Enjoying one moment at a time; Accepting hardships as the pathway to peace; Taking, as He did, this sinful world as it is, not as I would have it; Trusting that He will make all things right if I surrender to His Will; That I may be reasonably happy in this life and supremely happy with Him Forever in the next. Amen."

Psalm 86:1-5

"Incline your ear, O Lord, and answer me, for I am poor and needy. Preserve my life, for I am godly; save your servant, who trusts you-you are my God. Be gracious to me, O Lord for to you do I cry all the day. Gladden the soul of your servant, for to you, O Lord, do I lift up my

soul. For you, O Lord, is good and forgiving, abounding in steadfast love to all who call upon you. Give ear, O Lord, to my prayer; listen to my plea for grace. In the day of my trouble I call upon you for you to answer me."

Psalm 18:6, 16-19

"In my distress I called upon the Lord; to my God I cried for help. From his temple he heard my voice, and my cry to him reached his ears. He sent from on high, he took me; he drew me out of many waters. He rescued me from my strong enemy and from those who hated me, for they were too mighty for me. They confronted me in the day of calamity, but the Lord was my support. He brought me out into a broad place; he rescued me, because he delighted in me."

We all experience distress at some point in our lives. It is all about how we act upon the things that stress us. It is said that by the means of God and giving ourselves to His faith helps us. We are His children and He loves us, no matter the mistakes or mishaps we get ourselves into. It is important to realize that the Lord supports you no matter what happens in your everyday personal life, no matter the choices and decisions you make. You must have faith the He cares for you deeply, which should inspire you to pour your heart directly into Him.

How to Overcome Obstacles in Your Journey of Emotional Healing

Throughout our life, we will come across numerous types of obstacles, some tougher than we think we are able to adequately handle. We all need to realize that each of these obstacles serve a purpose. They provide us with the ability to develop further as individuals. Every obstacle is also a choice, a choice in the way we respond to whatever the obstacle may be. Instead of seeing it as a block in the road or the end of a tunnel, we need to learn to envision these as opportunities to act in loving ways, to forgive ourselves and others and to practice a sense of gratitude. It is crucial to learn how to navigate our way through impediments, but this can be quite the feat when one doesn't know properly how to do so.

Different Types of Obstacles

The obstacles that we all inevitably face in life are sorted into three categories and they can either fuel or inhibit you from reaching your goals and enjoying your life's journey.

Personal Obstacles – These kinds of obstacles are ones that deal with our state of mind, behavior and psychology. Included in this are crippling emotions and fears, limiting belief systems and habits that are unhelpful in nature. We allow these obstacles overwhelm our lives in debilitating ways that keep us from moving forward. The following are some things that we tend to do even without realizing it. They keep us from being better individuals, but we are so caught up in them that we do not see the harm.

- Complaining
- Excuses

- Not taking responsibility
- No urgency
- Time constraint issues
- Pessimism
- Un-organization
- Need to be perfect
- Procrastination
- Feeling of unworthiness
- Fear of failing
- Fear of imminent changes
- Lack of skill set
- Lack of passion or desire
- Lack of knowledge or desire to acquire it
- Lack of discipline
- Lack of patience
- Lack of pain

It is important to take the time and identify your own personal defects that are causing obstacles in your life right now, so you can take steps to make the best better!

Social Obstacles – These types of obstacles are those that deal with those who do not cooperate with your needs or wants or go out of their way to sabotage your life. There are going to be people that are in your life that are not quite competent enough to fulfill their responsibilities towards you either. It is important that you are able to identify your needs to other individuals, no one can read minds. Communicating effectively also strengthens your bond with your current and future relationships throughout your life. Where some people steer wrong is the fact that they get into the mindset that they can control other people's actions and decisions. Influence others by actually understanding their needs and this will help you through the social obstacles that could come your way at any time.

Environmental Obstacles – These types of obstacles are those that are unexpected and mainly unplanned for, situations that one usually has no control over. Because these circumstances come out of nowhere, we become very emotionally distraught over it and are not right away equipped to deal with things appropriately at times. It is good in these situations to have a backup plan before bad things occur. But we cannot make a detailed plan about anything that might happen. That keeps us in a trapped way of being able to live freely. This is where something known as 'Murphy's Law' comes into play. This law states *"anything that can go wrong, will go wrong at the worst possible time, all the time when you least expect it. So what are you going to do about it?"* When you take the time to plan into the future, you must gather knowledge of understanding situations and the consequences on how we decide to act on them. Designing possible plans to deal with the future allows you to also seek additional resources that you may need later. Is it important to develop a 360 degree way of thinking about circumstances of life? This way utilizes insight, foresight and hindsight when making important decisions.

The following are the steps of how to successfully conduct yourself when it comes to barriers that stand in your way.

Acceptance – We all no too well that the issues that shadow our lives do not just go away on their own. We either have to work through them or choose to ignore them and turn our back on our problems. If we decide to avoid obstacles, they may lessen to an extent but never actually go away, which leaves potholes in the roadway of our lives that we constantly have to steer away from or confront head on. They can prevent us from continuing forward, which is what no one wants. But, if we decide to confront our issues, we can start the process of working our way through it, which will make it evaporate over time. There first step is to accept that there IS an issue to begin with. This is the only way that one can get into the mindset of making the necessary changes to resolve the problem, no matter how big or small it may be.

Lessen emotion – Emotional meltdowns are natural when it comes to obstacles bombarding our lives. No matter how upset one becomes, emotions and their reactions are quite counterproductive and keep us from the real motive at hand. It is important for adults to take time out occasionally during these times, because it might not be possible to efficiently take care of an issue. Before having a crying fit, it is better to take time to set aside your emotions and look into yourself. What makes you a good person? How can YOU solve this problem that has fallen into your lap? Seeking wisdom inside yourself helps one get a clearer state of mind to create a plan to resolve whatever problems you are currently facing. Instead of being all caught up in the emotions you feel about the situation, we can better grasp the circumstances from a better perspective to identify what to really do.

Stop the blame – When it comes to absorbing difficult situations, there are many of us that typically go right into laying the blame on someone or something else. We need to have faith that everything happens for a reason. Blaming others or ourselves for certain happenings does nothing but keeping us rolling backwards and stuck under the issue rather than conquering it.

Take time for perspective – Our minds are sometimes our worst enemy and they warp what is happening into something way worse than how things actually are. At times, we make bigger deals over small issues than what they are truly cracked up to be, which can be unhealthy not just for us but for those closest to us too.

5 important questions to ask yourself – When an obstacle of any kind comes up in your life, it is important to step aside for a second and ask yourself the following questions:

1) What can I change?
2) What can't I change?
3) How can I grasp an understanding regarding the circumstances at hand?
4) What practices can help me through the obstacle?
5) What is the lesson regarding this situation?

By taking the time to answer these questions thoroughly, one can get better clearance as to what they should do to overcome the obstacle at hand. It also lets us gain the clarity to manage a situation from a better mental state of mind, rather than from an emotional stand point. Ask yourself the above inquiries whenever you feel like your emotions are gaining momentum or you feel like you are spiraling out of control at any time.

Get Guidance – There are many times that we feel alone in our struggles. But, if we turn to others and tell them your issues, you would be surprised at just how many other people are experiencing the same issues you are or have in their past. Talking to a close friend or relative or maybe even a therapist can help you gain insight as to what you could possibly do in regards to your obstacle(s) that stand in your way from moving forward. Talking things out can also help you gain a clearer perspective of the situation at hand as well.

Questions to Ask Yourself when Defeating Obstacles

It is vital to know where to start when catastrophic situations occur. The following are crucial questions when you are trying to find a beginning point to take on your obstacles head on.

Question the issue

- What are the symptoms of the problem at hand?
- How do you know that this information is completely accurate?

Question the Core of the Issues

- How and where did this problem generate?
- What or who keeps this problem an ongoing issue?

Identify Details

- When did the problem occur?
- How did the issue happen?
- Where did this issue take place?

Determine the Possible Consequences

- What will occur if you choose to avoid that problem at hand?
- When could it become a bigger issue or will it at all?
- What things would lead to certain outcomes?
- How will this all affect you in the short and long term?
- How will this all affect your life in the general sense?
- Could choosing to resolve this issue cause other problems?

Learn to Take Control

- Which behaviors of other people can you control?
- What part(s) of the issue at hand can you actually control?

- What aspects of the problem can't you get control of?
- How do you think you should respond if you think you cannot control the situation?
- How could you adapt to the situation and the changes that are likely to occur if you learn you cannot control it in any manner?

Get Some Perspective

- What do you expect to come from this problem?
- How are your expectations fueling the problem, if they are?
- Are they any other points of view you have yet to consider?
- Is there anyone else that has successfully defeated the same issue?

175

- What can you learn from other individuals who have already overcome these types of issues?

Broaden your Horizons when it comes to Options

- Is there anything you could do differently?
- Is there anyone that could help you through the issues you have?
- Is there anywhere you have yet to look for possible solutions?
- How will you know when your problems at hand have been resolved?
- What are your aspects for a successful journey through the issue?

How to Regain Confidence and Embrace your Inner Self

Those that have been through a type of traumatic event tend to have ever-lasting effects on our mental psyche as well as emotionally. Even though those who have been through some tough stuff have had time to heal in some manner, but they never truly gain their sense of self-confidence back from how it was before. This chapter is full of ideas and tips to help you regain that great sense of confidence and embrace your inner self, the you that you were before life's crappy situation(s).

For those that have suffered through the effects of trauma, they feel quite vulnerable and feel out of control in many aspects of their personal and public lives. These tips are meant to help you take back your life and get you in the saddle with the reigns right in your hands!

Create and get onto a regular every day schedule – No matter what you have been through, it is important to get the aspects of your life that you CAN control back on track as soon as possible. Eating normally, driving, going to work and exercising every day can give you a sense of normalcy, which will provide room to think normal once again. These 'normal' and routine activities will slowly get you back on track to living in a successful life, which will fuel the confidence boost.

Remember that what has happened to you does not define you – Once you have experienced any type of trauma one can become easily haunted for a long period of time. It may take some time, but one must eventually realize that your past does not define you in any way, shape or form.

Learn to forgive yourself as well as others who have hurt you – This is not saying you HAVE to forgive anyone. But you should forgive them for you and your own well-being. Forgiveness can actually liberate you in ways that negativity could never do. Resentment can fill up your soul in negative ways, so why not replace it with forgiveness for yourself. Forgiving anyone is about you, not whoever probably does not deserve that forgiveness. Ensure that you eventually release all that bad energy, for your sake!

Ensure time for self-care – It is important, especially in the after effects of trauma, to take care of yourself both mentally and physically. Partake in things that take care of your need, whether it is eating better, meditating or exercising daily.

Get rid of negative patterns of thought – Meditation assists with this tip extremely and is also known as negative thought replacement. It was created to reduce your negative and depressive thoughts. Making positive thinking patterns a habit will ensure that it sticks with you for a long time to come. When negative things come to haunt your mind, learn to tell yourself positive phrases or words to replace those bad thoughts. It does take some dedicated time and work, but replacing those types of thoughts will help you boost your self confidence in no time!

Do not lose touch with friends – After traumatic events, some people in your life will choose to avoid you to save themselves from awkward situations with you, mainly because they do not know what to say to make you feel better. What they don't realize is that is when people need those closest to them the MOST. Those who have gone through tough experiences need to learn to communicate the best they can to their friends what they would like from them.

Keep up with your favorite activities or attempt new hobbies – It all depends on the kind of traumatic event you have been through, you may not feel up to going out on dates or with friends. But it is important to partake in other activities like shopping at the mall and other activities that do not involve pressure of any kind. Joining a church group or other social event that interests you will help keep your mind off of the traumatic event as well as gets you hopefully talking to other people.

Learn to trust again – Traumatic events can naturally prevent us from being trusting of other people and situations. This especially goes towards people who hurt you. It takes time and patience, but it is very crucial to eventually move past this road block, otherwise it will always hold you back. You must put some faith into people and circumstances. Living life with barriers is not actually living. You will then become angry and discouraged with your life. Which leads to an even worse mental turmoil? Learn to reframe your state of mind to be wary, but to trust.

Exercise – Whether you did or didn't before, performing physical activity on a daily basis will help you feel better about yourself, as well as help you look better inside and out, which is a definite confidence booster!

Practice the ways of relaxation – Learning to deep breath, relax your muscles, meditate, pray, listen to music and doing things that help decrease bad thoughts by blocking out petty distractions will in the long run assist you in reducing negative sensations and positive feelings will increase, fueling that confidence!

Take some time to volunteer – Helping other besides yourself within your community will assist you in feeling important and show you that you do have something to offer other people.

Keep yourself updated with your case and information – If the traumatic event that you endured happened to be a criminal act, ensure that you stay on top of the things happening within your case. Even the tiniest details can help solve you case if remains open.

When it comes to building confidence, it is vital to take care of yourself and be considerate of what you have been through. Getting better in a positive manner takes quite a bit of time, where you will need to learn to be patient with yourself and the progress you make. No matter how tiny the step, progress is indeed progress! You may not be proud of who you are now or right after a traumatic event, but ensure that you are making strides to once again have the confidence to take on life with a full potential purpose!

Conclusion

Congratulations and thank for making it through to the end of *Emotional Healing: Coping with Emotional and Psychological Trauma*. I hope that the contents of this book changed your mindset in a positive manner in terms of finding yourself through life's inevitable tragedies and traumas that we are all susceptible in facing at any given time.

I hope that you found the information valuable in terms of providing self-help tips and tricks, and that you will share your new-found knowledge with anyone who is also struggling to make emotional ends meet.

The next step is to put what you have acquired from the pages of this book and put them into action! No amount of healing comes from binge watching Netflix and throwing a 24/7 pity party.

Life is a bitch, but you have to make it yours! And it is very much possible for anyone, including you, if you step up and take initiative to change your life TODAY. Each and every human being has the power to change the world, but you must start with yourself to truly make a difference. You can't go around making the world yours when you feel like you are drowning.

So, what are you waiting for? Get up and start emotional healing yourself RIGHT NOW.

CHAKRAS

Chakras for Beginners, Awaken Your Internal
Positive Energy, Healing, Spiritual Growth,
Balancing, Essential Oil for the Chakras

MELISSA A. HOLLOWAY

Chakras

Chakras for Beginners, Awaken Your Internal Positive Energy, Healing, Spiritual Growth, Balancing, Essential Oil for the Chakras

By Melissa Anna Holloway

Table of Contents

Introduction

Chakras are energy centers within' the body. They are often talked about in spirituality and within' energy healing, and for good reason. It is likely that you have heard the term "chakras" before, and the curiosity about what they are has drawn you here to learn more. Chakras are a wonderful thing to learn about, as knowing how to work with them and heal them has the ability to bring an enormous amount of peace, harmony, and happiness into your life.

In this book, you are going to learn all about the seven main chakras. You will learn about what they are, where they are and what they represent. You will also learn about how you can heal them, and what sorts of natural remedies you can use with each. Within' this book you will learn about the value of balancing the chakras and how you can do so, as well as what you can expect both when they are balanced and out of balance. By the end, you will be confident in your knowledge about the seven primary chakras and how they can serve you in your life. Each chapter has been written for your reading pleasure, and the knowledge within' this book is directed towards beginners. That being said, you will learn everything you need to know from the bottom up, and by the end, you will know exactly how you can work with your own chakras to heal and empower your life. The knowledge you gain within' this book will assist you in having a greater understanding of yourself, your energy body, and the world around you. Please take your time and enjoy your reading experience.

Chapter 1: What Are Chakras?

Prior to being able to actually use the chakras for healing and other energy work, it is important to understand what they are and where they come from. When you are able to understand the history and origin of chakras, as well as what they are exactly, you will have a greater ability to understand why they are important and how they can help you. Establishing this foundation around the chakra knowledge will create a better basis for you to learn all about them throughout the rest of this book.

History and Origins

Back between 1500 and 500 BC within' the oldest Indian text of the Vedas, there was writing about the chakras. These chakras, then spelled "cakra", have also been referenced in other texts and history including the Cudamini Upanishad, the Shri Jabala Darshana Upanishad, the Shandilya Upanishad and the

Yoga-Shikka Upanishad. The knowledge about the sophisticated chakra system passed through the Ino-European people through oral tradition. These people were also called Aryan. Traditionally, the chakra system was part of Eastern philosophy; however, New Age authors resonated deeply with the idea and made it more readily available to modern people through their text.

What Are Chakras?

When you look at the very definition of a chakra, it is a spinning disk or a wheel. Essentially, a chakra is known to be a spinning disk on the human body that churns energy through it. The chakras run along the length of your spine, starting at the "root" chakra at the base of your spine, all the way to your "crown" chakra at the top of your head. There are seven primary chakras that run along this length of your body, though in some more sophisticated and in-depth texts you will read that there are as many as 114 throughout the entire body and energy field.

The primary chakras focused upon in spirituality and energy work and healing are the seven that run along the length of your spine. These chakras directly associate with the health of the physical body, mind, and emotions of a person. Because of this, many practices such as energy healing and yoga work closely with the chakras to create a powerful state of wellbeing for everyone who takes the time to engage in these activities.

What Do Chakras Do?

Expanding on the idea of chakras being spinning lights of energy over primary areas on the body, you can then grow to realize that each one has a unique purpose directly associated with the wellbeing of the body. Essentially, they govern the way we psychologically experience life when we are affected by mental and emotional stimuli. Each spinning disc contributes to our overall wellbeing, and we can directly experience what our chakra experiences, whether it is open, closed, balanced or unbalanced, active or inactive, so on and so forth. When you work with these chakras to have them operating in a healthy flow, you will find that your wellbeing physically, emotionally and mentally is much more positive overall. You can drastically alter your state of being through the chakras, and therefore working with them has a powerful ability to heal your energetic, physical and spiritual beings. When you release any blockages within' the chakra and balance them so that they work in healthy flow, you give yourself the ability to flow easily through a healthy, enlightened and balanced existence. The balance within' our chakras directly correlates with the balance in our own personal lives, physically, mentally and emotionally.

Working with them can assist you in eliminating many unwanted ailments you may be suffering from.

What Else Do I Need to Know About Chakras?

Each chakra is located in a different spot along your spine and serves a different purpose. They also affect different organs and correlate with different ailments. Each one has its own color. They also directly relate to their own set of emotions, feelings, and behaviors. Each one can be worked on to heal the ailments that directly associate with it, once you realize which one is unbalanced or out of alignment.

The chakras are a very sophisticated map of the energy body and directly affect our physical, mental and emotional bodies as well. They were first depicted in text sometime between 1500 of 500 BC in some of the oldest texts in the world.

Chakras offer a powerful opportunity for you to learn how you can balance your body and heal many ailments that you may struggle or suffer fro. When you do, you will likely find that your entire wellbeing is much better off for it.

Chapter 2: The Seven Chakras

As you learned in the previous chapter, there are seven primary chakras that you should consider. While some people believe there are up to 114, most people simply focus on these primary seven. Each chakra governs its own set of feelings, emotions, organs, and behaviors. They also have their own color and placement on the bottom. Within' this chapter, we are going to go deeper into the knowledge on each of the seven chakras. We will start with the one at the bottom of your spine known as the "root chakra" and work our way up to the one at the top of your spine called the "crown chakra". This order takes us from the first to the seventh chakra. Along the way, you will learn all that you need to know about each one.

The Root Chakra

The first of all of the seven chakras is the Root Chakra. This bright red chakra is located at the base of your spine, between your legs. In some texts or teachings, this chakra is associated with an Earthy brown tone, instead of a red one.

The Root Chakra is responsible for feeling grounded and stable in your life, as well as feeling a sense of security. The most common signal that this chakra is unaligned is a feeling of anxiety. You can experience this symptom whether this chakra is under or over active. If you are experiencing an underactive Root Chakra, you will also experience feelings of being unsafe or afraid in your life. If it is overactive, you may be feeling stuck in your ways or struggle to accept transition or change within your life. Either way, the best method for balancing this chakra is to meditate and practice grounding techniques. In doing so, you will help alleviate many of the ailments that arise with it. This chakra directly associates with the organs such as your kidney, reproductive glands and organs, and your spine. If you are experiencing any difficulties such as kidney infections or pain, difficulty reproducing or with reproductive hormones, or pain in your spinal column, it may be due to your Root Chakra being misaligned. You can likely restore balance to your chakra and experience reduced stress in any of these systems.

The Sacral Chakra

The second of the seven chakras is the Sacral Chakra. This chakra is located above the pelvis in between your hips. This chakra resonates with the color orange.

The Sacral Chakra is responsible for your passion, sexuality and your creativity. When you are experiencing an underactive Sacral Chakra, you may struggle to create, feel apathetic or rigid, or feel as though you are closed off from intimacy. When this chakra is extremely underactive, you may experience not only a lack of intimacy physically but emotionally as well.

Alternatively, if this chakra is overactive you may feel as though you are extremely sexual to the point that you may be considered somewhat of a sex addict. You may also find that you tend to become emotionally attached easily, as well. Either way, you need to take the time to balance your Sacral Chakra. You can do so through meditation, mindfulness, and using some of the natural methods discussed later within' this book.

This chakra is directly associated with the organs such as your gallbladder, adrenal glands, immune system, waste organs, metabolism, and your spleen. When you are experiencing ailments within' any of these chakras, you should take the time to bring balance back to your Sacral Chakra. In doing so, you will likely eliminate a large amount of your negative side effects and symptoms.

The Solar Plexus Chakra

The third chakra is the Solar Plexus Chakra and once again it's placement may seem obvious. It is located at the solar plexus, just above the belly button. This golden yellow chakra is a powerful one that resonates deeply with many areas of our lives.

The Solar Plexus Chakra is responsible for feelings of self-confidence, will, personal power and force. When you are feeling any misalignment within' the chakra, the emotional drawbacks will be difficult to manage. With an underactive Solar Plexus Chakra, you will find that you are feeling powerless, timid, or under confident within' yourself. If you are feeling low self-esteem, it is often associated with this chakra, as well. You may also lack direction or purpose within' your life. If this chakra is overactive, you may find that you are potentially aggressive or domineering and that you tend to try and be the "boss" of situations. Either is something that you should not strive for. Bringing balance to this chakra will assist you in feeling more confident and empowered without feeling as though you have to become overpowering.

The organs associated with the Solar Plexus Chakra include the upper spine, liver, stomach, pancreas, and metabolism. When this chakra is unbalanced, you may experience pain or ailments within' any of these systems. When you bring balance to the chakra, it is likely that each will function more efficiently and that your overall wellbeing will be enhanced by it.

The Heart Chakra

The fourth of the seven chakras is the Heart Chakra. This chakra is associated with the color green and is located directly in the center of your rib cage. As you may assume, it is located exactly where your heart is. Some people call this chakra the "Heart Center". The two appear to be used interchangeably throughout text regarding energy healing and the energy body. In this book, we will call it the Heart Chakra.

The Heart Charka is primarily responsible for feelings of love and compassion. When you are experiencing an underactive Heart Chakra, you may find that you struggle to feel love or compassion for people and things in your life. You may even struggle to experience these emotions for yourself. If your Heart Chakra is overactive, you may find that you love and give compassion freely to the point that you become clingy or overly affectionate towards people. If either of these situations is happening, you need to balance your Heart Chakra. You can do so by taking the time to go inward and discover what is causing you to be one way or the other. Often, we are affected by emotional experiences in our lives that cause us to be extremely cold or extremely affectionate towards others.

This chakra directly correlates with the heart organ, the lungs, and the thymus. If you are experiencing ailments in either of these, you may wish to do some energy balancing work with your heart chakra to restore balance and harmony within' them. Doing so may bring relief from any ailments that bother you.

The Throat Chakra

As you may have guessed, the fifth chakra which is known as the Throat Chakra is located within' the throat. The color that correlates with this chakra is a bright and vibrant blue color. Typically, it is seen as more of a light blue color, though you may see it represented as nearly any shade of blue.

This chakra is responsible for honest communication and ease of self-expression. When this chakra is underactive, you may experience symptoms of being withdrawn, or even frustration, sadness, or anger due to feeling as though you are not speaking your truth. Alternatively, if it is overactive you may speak excessively and fail to filter yourself to the point that you may be seen as bossy or rude. Or, you may be a bad listener and you may listen merely for the opportunity to speak back. When you are experiencing either of these sets of symptoms, it is important that you take the time to develop a mindfulness practice and allow yourself to regain control over your voice. You should work on being honest if you are feeling as though you are hiding your truth, or you should work on keeping thoughts to yourself or learning to censor yourself if you are giving information or opinions too freely to the point that it is inhibiting your life.

The Throat Chakra is associated with the respiratory system, thyroid, and all organs that are associated with your throat and mouth. If you are experiencing any ailments with these organs, you may be experiencing physical symptoms of an unbalanced chakra. The most commonly reported symptom is feeling as though you have a lump in your throat. You can eliminate or ease these symptoms by restoring balance to your throat chakra and speaking your truth without over speaking.

The Third Eye Chakra

The Third Eye Chakra is located directly between and slightly above your eyebrows. This chakra is indicated by the color indigo and is considered to be the sixth of the seven chakras. For many, this is the most popularly recognized chakra as it is spoken about in many texts and spiritual teachings.

The Third Eye Chakra is responsible for bringing connection to intuition, psychic vision, and insight. When you are experiencing an underactive chakra, you may struggle to stay in touch with your intuitive side, or you may feel lost and as though you are wandering through life. Alternatively, if it is overactive, you may feel paranoid about your gut instincts and overanalyze things that are completely ordinary in life. To balance this chakra, you will want to meditate. Your meditation can have the intention of relaxing the chakra, or of opening it up depending on whether it is underactive or overactive. As a result, it should bring you back into a healthy flow where you can acknowledge and listen to your intuition without developing any fear or paranoia around the information that it brings you.

Physically, the Third Eye Chakra is associated with your pineal gland, pituitary gland, eyes, hormones and your brain. If you are experiencing misalignment in this chakra, you could experience a number of ailments with either of these organs. You may get headaches behind your eyes or experience disturbances in vision, you may get frequent headaches or "brain fog", you could experience hormonal changes that disrupt your wellbeing, or you could experience overactive or underactive pineal and pituitary glands. Bringing balance back to this chakra should be able to assist you in healing these ailments.

The Crown Chakra

Located on top of your scalp at the very top of your head, your Crown Chakra corresponds with the color purple. However, some people believe this chakra corresponds with the color white. You can use either one that resonates with you, but for this book and these teachings we are going to use purple. This chakra is considered the seventh of the seven chakras.

The Crown Chakra is responsible for assisting people with wisdom, being in attunement with the universe, and connecting to the spiritual realm. When this chakra is underactive, you may feel disconnected from spirit and as though you are making a number of foolish decisions. When it is overactive, you may feel as though you have your head in the clouds and you have difficulty connecting with reality. Neither of these are positive symptoms to have, so it is important that you bring balance back to the chakra to heal them. When it is functioning optimally, you will be able to have a healthy connection to the spiritual realm while still feeling firmly grounded in your life. If the chakra is overactive, you will want to ground yourself to bring yourself back down to Earth. If it is underactive, you will want to meditate and set the intention to reopen your ability to interact with the spiritual realm.

This chakra is responsible for governing the brain, the pineal gland, your biological cycles, and the spinal cord. When it is out of balance, you may experience ailments to any one of these. Your pineal gland may not function well, you may struggle to sleep well or you may sleep too much, you may experience pain in your spinal area or you may experience "brain fog" or frequent headaches. If you are noticing a number of these ailments or any single one that appears to be persistent and difficult to manage, you may want to consider healing and balancing your Crown Chakra. It may be unbalanced and bringing a lack of wellbeing to any of these areas.

When you see a map of the chakras, you may notice that they are coordinated in the colors of the rainbow. This knowledge is wonderful to note as it will assist you in remembering which color is associated with which chakra. Remember, red starts at the base and purple is at the top. Each chakra has its own color, emotions, behaviors and organs associated with it. When either is underactive or overactive or otherwise misaligned, you may experience symptoms associated with anything that your particular chakra is responsible for. If you are experiencing specific symptoms, you may want to revisit the chakras to see which one associates with where your symptoms are being felt. Then, you can do work with that chakra to bring peace and harmony to it and hopefully alleviate some or all of your symptoms.

Chapter 3: Balancing Chakras

It is very important that you invest time in balancing your chakras in order to keep them operating smoothly and efficiently. In the previous chapter, you saw some of the symptoms you may experience when your chakras are not operating in perfect harmony. You can often alleviate many of these symptoms by balancing your chakras. You should do it on a daily basis to maintain balance, although you still may discover that occasionally one chakra may be operating more or less than the others. In this case, you will want to specifically focus on that chakra either through one of the balancing strategies or natural healing remedies provided within' this book in later chapters.

What Does It Mean to Balance a Chakra?

When your chakras are imbalanced it means that they are operating in a state that is either considered underactive or overactive. When you are new to chakras, you may think that to balance your chakra means to open it. Sometimes, this isn't the case, however. If your chakra is overactive, for example, you do not want to further open it. Instead, you want your chakras flowing at an optimal balance that allows them to work healthfully and not too much or too little.

To balance a chakra actually means that you are ensuring that it is receiving and transmitting energy at an optimal rate. You want your chakra to be flowing efficiently enough to do its job, but not so efficiently that it does it too well. You can do so by either opening it up more or closing it more based on how the chakra itself is functioning.

Why Is It Important to Balance Chakras?

To get a better idea of why balance is important, let's think about your heart organ for a minute. When your heart is functioning optimally, it spreads blood evenly throughout your body. When it is underactive, however, you may get diagnosed with low blood pressure and it brings around a series of ailments. Alternatively, if you are dealing with a heart that pushes out blood too efficiently then you may get diagnosed with high blood pressure. Again, this condition can bring about a series of ailments. As with everything in life, balance is highly important.

Chakras that are balanced function optimally and create a space that allows you to gain maximum benefit from your chakras. They are able to serve their purpose efficiently without serving it too much. You can feel the healthy flow from chakras that are functioning properly. They contribute to your overall well-being and keep you living in a place of peace and harmony that allows for you to absorb as much positive energy and experiences from your life and environment as possible.

How Can I Balance My Chakras?

There are many ways to balance your chakras and in the chapters following this one you are going to learn more specifically how you can do so. In general, though, the balancing of chakras has a lot to do with setting the intention to balance them. Many of the activities you use to balance your chakras are merely you using tools and skills in order to bring them back into balance. When you set the intention to balance your chakras, your entire efforts become a lot more efficient. Knowing that, you should always set the intention to balance your chakra before you start working on it. Do not set the intention to open it or close it, because you may set the wrong intention and thus create a greater imbalance in your chakra. Instead, set the intention that the universe gives it the best amount of life force energy to assist it in being balanced and working for your optimal benefit.

Some of the ways you are going to learn to work with your chakras include meditation, crystal healing, affirmations and natural remedies that can be used within' the chakras. Other ways you may wish to work with the chakras include through prayer, yoga, and gentle exercise. You can even go to places where professional energy healing is done, such as through reiki. When your body is healthy, so too will your mind and spirit be healthy. The same goes in all directions. Achieving an overall state of wellbeing comes from nurturing and caring for all of your energy bodies. The more you can take care of these centers, the better you are going to feel in general.

It is incredibly important for you to balance your chakras. You should also take the time to heal them whenever necessary. As you practice working with your chakras more often, you will develop a greater intuition around them and you will know when they need your attention or assistance. As a result, you will be able to pick the perfect vehicles for you to balance or remedy them. Doing so will assist you in creating a perfect inner harmony and balance in your life. There are many ways that you can balance and heal your chakras, how you choose to do so will largely depend on what your specific desire is and how you need to achieve it in the way that will be most optimal to your balancing or healing needs. The more practiced you become, the easier it will be for you to continue balancing and healing your chakras.

Remember, the balancing process is an ongoing thing. You cannot balance your chakras once and expect them to be balanced forever. You will need to spend time balancing your chakras on a daily basis in order to ensure that they stay balanced. Of course, if you miss a few days here and there it won't matter terribly much, as long as you are staying in tune with your chakras and are able to take time aside to rebalance them and work with them when they need it. When you invest this time in healing and maintaining your chakras, you will notice a world of difference in regards to your overall health and wellbeing. Your chakras are much more important to your overall wellbeing than you may presently realize. Balancing them is a powerful way to maintain them and ensure that they continue serving your highest good.

Chapter 4: Crystal Healing

Balancing your chakras can be done in many ways, and typically you will want to use several methods in order to restore and maintain balance within' your chakras. A very common way to bring balance to your chakras is with crystals. You can use crystals in many ways, and they have the wonderful advantage of not requiring you to do too much to gain the benefits from them. You can keep them nearby, in your pocket, or wear them as jewelry to gain the benefits from these healing stones. You may also specifically work with them such as through meditation or affirmations to assist you in bringing balance to your chakras.

Crystals You Can Use

Each chakra has its own set of crystals associated with it. The following lists show you the most common crystals associated with each chakra. Please note these lists are not exhaustive. You will find more in-depth information below about using other crystals, and picking which crystals to use.

Root Chakra Stones

- Hematite
- Garnet
- Black Tourmaline
- Zircon
- Black Obsidian
- Smoky Quartz
- Jet
- Red Jasper

Sacral Chakra Stones

- Carnelian
- Blue-Green Turquoise
- Copper

- Blue-Green Fluorite
- Imperial Topaz
- Orange Calcite
- Vanadinite

Solar Plexus Chakra

- Citrine
- Yellow Jasper
- Amber
- Gold Tiger's Eye
- Golden Calcite
- Yellow Appatite

Heart Chakra

- Rose Quartz
- Pink Danburite
- Vesuvianite

- Lepidolite

- Watermelon Tourmaline

- Jade

- Malachite

- Rosasite

- Pink/Rubellite Tourmaline

- Green Aventurine

- Cobaltian Calcite

Throat Chakra

- Blue Calcite

- Sodalite

- Angelite

- Blue Chalcedony

- Blue Lace Agate

- Aquamarine

- Amazonite

- Blue Turquoise

- Chrysocolla

- Celestite

- Blue Kyanite

Third Eye Chakra

- Tanzanite

- Azurite

- Lapis Lazuli

Crown Chakra

- Quartz

- Herkimer Diamond

- Selenite

- White Howlite

- White Hemimorphite

- White Danburite

- White Topaz

- White Calcite

- Amethyst

- Apophyllite

Picking Crystals

There are many more crystals beyond what was listed above, and you may wish to use any number of them. Alternatively, you may struggle to decide exactly which one to use since there are so many to choose from. There are many ways to pick your crystals, to be exact. However, there are a few things you should consider to help you pick exactly which one can benefit you for the specific purpose that you are searching for.

First, you should understand that your intuition will often draw you to exactly what you need in your life. This is true in two ways: one, you will want to choose the one you are most drawn to. It is likely that you need this in your life. Two, you should also consider the stone you are most drawn *away* from. These often carry an additional important piece of information that you need to consider, as well.

Next, if you are choosing stones that are not on the list but you want one for a specific chakra, look for stones that correlate with the colors of the chakras. Remember, though, the root chakra can be associated with red, black or brown. The throat chakra is typically associated with lighter blues and the third eye chakra is the darker blues. The crown chakra can be associated with purple or white. When you choose a stone, you can choose based off of the color to pick one for each chakra, or for the specific chakra you want to consider.

Another way you can pick your stone is based on its unique healing abilities. Although each stone falls under a specific chakra, they do have their own independent abilities. For example, the amethyst stone is amazing for protection and the quartz stone is wonderful for clarification.

Still, both are used for the crown chakra. The same rings true for virtually every stone, so if you have a specific ailment you may wish to find a stone that will work specifically with that ailment.

How to Use Crystals

Using crystals is easy, and there are many ways that you can do so. Crystals are one of the most versatile healing formats for the energy body and can be used with intention and then in almost any way to assist in healing. The following are some of the most common ways to use them.

Meditate with Them

One way that you can really gain a lot of benefit from crystals is to meditate with them. You can hold them in your hand or simply keep them nearby. Often when you are meditating with crystals you will want to keep your gaze on them, as opposed to closing your eyes. However, you can still close your eyes if you desire. If you want to work with all of your chakras, you may consider lying on your back and placing a stone over each chakra and then lying that way for a while until you feel as though your chakras have been aligned and balanced once again.

Keep Them Nearby

Crystals have powerful energies and you can gain the energies simply by having them around. You can keep a piece of a crystal nearby, keep a small bowl of them, or otherwise keep them in your presence. You may want to place crystals in certain places to bring certain energies to those places. For example, you may wish to put black obsidian by the door to keep negative energies out of your house, and rose quartz by your bed to keep you peaceful and calm when you are sleeping. There are many different crystals that you can keep nearby, depending on what you are trying to achieve. Some prefer to put them out them put them away when they are done, whereas others prefer to keep them out permanently.

Wear Them

A very common and powerful way to use crystals is to have them resting against your skin. You can do this by wearing them as jewelry. You can wear earrings, necklaces, bracelets, rings or any other form of jewelry with these crystals within' them and wear them. Some people wear them only with a specific purpose and others wear them on a daily basis. It is said that when crystals are directly against your skin, you absorb the maximum benefit from them.

Keep Them in Your Pocket

If you are not one to wear jewelry, you may wish to keep the stones in your pocket or in a medicine bag instead. This way, you can keep them nearby and still have them to use. Some people even like to carry around worry stones, which are crystals that you keep in your pocket and when you need a stronger "dose" of their energy, you can simply rub your thumb or fingers through the indentation in the stone.

There are many reasons and uses for crystals, just as there are many ways you can use them. Some people even allow them to "steep" in water and then drink the water to gain their benefits. Of course, you would want to make sure the crystal was clean before doing this. However, it goes to show that there are virtually limitless ways to gain the positive energies from these stones and gain the value that they have to offer. Crystals are one of the most powerful and useful natural healing "remedies" available, and pretty much everyone can benefit from their many uses. Whether you want a gentle rebalancing or

if you want to completely heal an unaligned
chakra, crystals can offer you a world of help.

Chapter 5: Spiritual Affirmations

The power of prayer and the power of spoken word are extremely powerful. You can use spoken word or affirmations to assist you in creating a balance within' your chakras and setting intentions for what you wish to achieve. You can use these affirmations either mentally or verbally and gain value from them, as the primary point is to release the intention for them into your life. Affirmations have been scientifically proven to assist in clearing and focusing the mind which can bring about a great deal of value when you are looking to heal your life.

What is an Affirmation?

Affirmations are short sayings or mantras that you can use on a regular basis to create a specific focus and intention in your life. Generally, you want to say an affirmation out loud and at least three times to gain benefit from it. The more you say it, the better they work. Additionally, you want to use a great deal of intention and emotion behind your affirmations. While you could simply say it, it is best if you say it with purpose and meaning. The more you believe in the affirmation, the more power it will have when it comes to balancing and healing your chakras and your life.

Which Affirmation Should I Use?

Each chakra has its own governing bodies, emotions, and symptoms; therefore, each chakra also has its own type of affirmations you would want to use with it. The following are affirmations that you can use specifically with each chakra.

The Root Chakra

"I am balanced in life"

"I am safe and secure"

"I am firmly grounded"

"I trust"

"I am responsible for my own body"

The Sacral Chakra

"I create freely"

"I have healthy feelings"

"I lovingly appreciate and accept myself as I am"

"I am loveable"

"I am strong"

The Solar Plexus Chakra

"I am enough"

"I take pride in my accomplishments and for who I am"

"I am confident"

"I am powerful"

"I honor and respect myself and my choices"

The Heart Chakra

"I love myself and the world around me"

"I open myself up to receive love, infinitely"

"I give love freely"

"My heart is full of love"

"I heal my heart and life with love"

The Throat Chakra

"I speak my truth effortlessly"

"I am honest with my words"

"I speak lovingly and kindly"

"I claim my own voice"

"My story is my own"

The Third Eye Chakra

"I am an intuitive being"

"I trust my intuition and inner guidance"

"I see the world clearly as it is"

"I see myself for who I truly am"

"I manifest all that I desire into my reality"

The Crown Chakra

"I am a divine being"

"I am connected to spirit"

"I am a limitless and infinite being"

"I am balanced"

"I am deeply connected to spirit and the universe"

Can I Use Other Affirmations?

The above affirmations are a wonderful idea of where to start, but you can certainly go ahead and create your own affirmations. In fact, creating your own affirmations is a wonderful way to increase the power behind your affirmations and therefore the effectiveness of them. The real power behind affirmations comes from believing in what you are saying. Therefore, when you create your own affirmations it becomes even easier to believe in what you are saying and gain value from them. Your affirmations can correlate to anything surrounding the chakra that you are intending to work with, or all of them if you intend to do so.

How Can I Increase the Effectiveness of Affirmations?

Of course, saying affirmations on its own is powerful. But, there are certainly ways to increase the amount of power behind saying them. For starters, having true meaning and purpose behind them is a good way. If you say an affirmation without meaning it, it may not work. Or, it may take longer to work because you must first develop the ability to believe in what you are saying. If you say it with conviction and belief from the get-go, you will increase the effectiveness.

Another way to increase the effectiveness of your affirmations is to say them out loud, especially in front of a mirror where you are looking at yourself. If you get into a power stance, you further increase the conviction behind them and therefore the power within' them. You can do so by putting your hands high in the air as if you were about to start cheering and then confidently say each affirmation to yourself. Then, you can physically see yourself commanding each affirmation and the confidence within' yourself. This further increases your ability to believe it, hold yourself accountable, and thus gain value from it.

Affirmations are a powerful speech method that enables you to change your life through spoken word. You can use affirmations for virtually anything, and you may even wish to use several at once. Ideally, you should use them on a regular basis, at least daily. The more you do, the more you will benefit from them.

Chapter 6: Meditations

Meditation is a strong and common way to bring balance to your life and body. Understandably, it also brings balance to your chakras. You can meditate in many ways to bring balance to the chakras, how exactly you do so will depend on your intention and your desired outcome from your meditation. In general, meditation is one of the most common methods for maintaining your chakras and keeping them in perfect balance. Most people prefer to meditate on a daily basis so that they can truly gain the most value from it.

Meditation itself is powerful for bringing balance to your mind, body, and spirit. However, there are chakra-specific meditations that you can do to bring alignment and balance to your chakras, as well. The following is a step-by-step tutorial on how you can meditate to heal your chakras or to simply maintain their balance.

Step One

Start by sitting down in a comfortable chair. Your feet should be firmly planted on the floor, and your spine should be tall and straight with your Crown Chakra reaching towards the sky. You can keep your hands gently relaxed on your lap for comfort. Even though the position of your body is important, make sure you are comfortable in maintaining it. There is no need to sit rigid and stiff. You can relax yourself into the position so that you can easily meditate.

Step Two

Start focusing on each part of your body and doing a "body scan" to really check in with yourself. Start at your feet and slowly work your way up through your shins, knees, thighs, glutes, abdominals, torso, arms, upper back, shoulders, neck, and then your head. Each time you move your focus, imagine that the stress and tension from that area slowly melt away and that it becomes completely relaxed. Set the intention for total relaxation.

Step Three

Meditating largely requires you to focus on your breath, and the same goes for a chakra meditation. Take the time now to start focusing on your breath. Do not force it, but become mindful over its flow. Allow it to become steady and deep, and try and breathe in through the nose and out through the mouth. If you discover that your awareness is drawing away from your body or your breath, gently bring it back and start focusing on your breath once again. Take a moment to visualize what it looks like as the oxygen fills your lungs and then transfers into your bloodstream and spreads out to all of your organs. Visualize the nourishing effect it has as it radiantly fills each organ and removes all of the toxins from your body each time that you breathe out.

Step Four

Now that you have completely relaxed and dropped into a meditative state, take the time to start visualizing the beat of your heart. See in your mind's eye how perfectly your body functions, and how it all works together harmoniously. Visualize the way your breath fulfills all of these areas of your body and how your breath gives the life force to your entire being. Continue to be still and mindful of your body and the sensations you are feeling.

Step Five

Now you should visualize something around you that represents life force energy. For some, this is a cloud or a light. You can use whatever feels right for you. You want to imagine that this life force energy is a golden yellow in color. You will want to visualize that you are breathing this in with each breath as it fully infuses with your body and your aura. As it does, imagine that your entire aura grows stronger and gets brighter with every single breath you take. Feel it being charged with the energy from the life force that surrounds you. Continue to do this gradually as the auric energy continues to get brighter and brighter. The energy should continue flowing in you and through you with each breath that you take.

Step Six

Now that you have visualized your body being charged and energized by the life force aura around you, you will want to start energizing each individual chakra in your body. To start, focus on your root chakra. Imagine that the energy is red and that it spins in a clockwise swirl around your root chakra. As you focus on it, imagine it getting stronger and brighter.

Imagine now that there is another energy source coming up from the Earth and feeding your chakra. As it does, imagine that it further charges and strengthens your root chakra. When your chakra is flowing effortlessly and the red light is strong and bright, you can move on to the next chakra.

Step Seven

Now you will want to do the same practice with your Sacral Chakra. Imagine that your chakra is glowing bright orange and the energy is flowing in a clockwise motion. As it spins and you take breaths in and out, imagine the energy getting stronger and brighter. The more you breathe the easier it spins and the easier it spins the brighter it gets. Keep doing this until the chakra is flowing fluidly and effortlessly.

Step Eight

Next is the Solar Plexus Chakra. Again, imagine that a bright golden yellow energy is in your solar plexus and that it is spinning clockwise. With each breath that you take in, the chakra spins smoother, and as it does, it glows brighter as well. You can continue breathing and relaxing into this chakra until it is flowing smooth and effortlessly.

Step Nine

Moving up the chakras, you arrive now at the Heart Chakra. Imagine the bright green energy of the chakra flowing clockwise as you breathe into it and it gains brightness and strength. Continue meditating on this chakra until it spins effortlessly and fluidly and the bright green light is powerful and vibrant.

Step Ten

Now you are at the Throat Chakra. You can imagine a bright lighter blue light in this chakra, and breathe into it as it spins clockwise. Imagine that each time you breathe in it glows brighter and each time you breathe out it glows even brighter. The brighter it gets, the easier it spins. The easier it spins, the more powerful it becomes and the brighter it gets.

Step Ten

You are now at your Third Eye Chakra. Here you can visualize a vibrant deep blue light spinning clockwise over your Third Eye. Imagine the light as it spins that it continues to grow brighter and stronger and that your energy grows more and more powerful. You can see that it is spinning even easier with each breath, until the point that it is completely balanced and flowing effortlessly.

Step Eleven

Finally, you arrive at the Crown Chakra. Here, you can visualize either a white light or a purple light. There, imagine it is spinning clockwise and that every time you breathe it gets stronger and spins more smoothly. At this time, you can also imagine that source above you will start connecting to your crown chakra through an energy rod and as you meditate on it, it gains power and strength. As it does, imagine it glowing brighter and brighter until it is vibrant and spinning freely.

Step Twelve

Imagine all of your seven chakras vibrantly glowing as it spins effortlessly and brings harmony and peace to everything around it. Each chakra is powerful and bringing you strength and balance into the rest of your body and the chakras around it. At this time if you notice any chakra is not feeling as balanced as the rest, and if you do you can spend some time increasing that chakra so that it flows evenly with the rest of them.

Step Thirteen

Finally, when you are done and you can visualize and feel that all of your chakras are balanced, you can end your meditation. You can now take the time to breathe deeply, inhale peace and positivity and exhale peace and positivity. Feel the love surrounding all of your chakras and the harmony that is within' your body. Take your time and really notice all of the energy feeding your energy body.

This meditation is something that you should attempt to do on a daily basis. When you do, you will keep each of your chakras operating healthfully and will be able to notice when either of them isn't as balanced as it should be. Doing this on a regular basis also sets you up to really gain a personalized idea on your chakras and how they influence and affect your life. You develop a sort of relationship with them and you will be able to tell when one is misaligned or feeling affected by the rest.

Meditation is a strategy that you should use on a daily basis, but especially when it comes to bringing balance and harmony to your body. Doing so will assist you in leading a healthier life with a more whole and positive wellbeing that will bring you to a higher state of being in your life.

Chapter 7: Natural Remedies

Just as each chakra is associated with organs, colors, behaviors, and emotions, they are also associated with their own unique healing energies. This chapter is going to assist you in gaining a greater understanding on how you can heal each chakra naturally. Doing so is a wonderful way to help rebalance misaligned chakras and bring harmony and peace to your energy body and, as a result, your physical body as well.

When You Should Use Natural Healing

Natural healing remedies are not necessary all of the time. They are remedies that you should use specifically if you want to focus on a certain element of a chakra. If you are struggling with a certain ailment or symptom of misalignment, then you will want to consider healing remedies associated with that chakra. Alternatively, if you are wanting to access the wisdom behind a chakra then you may wish to use a healing remedy associated with that chakra to assist you in doing so.

Healing remedies are not necessary otherwise. You do not need to use these for everyday maintenance of your chakras. Though, you can if you desire. More specifically, you want to reserve these for times that you want to specifically focus on healing the chakras and balancing ones that may be extremely misaligned.

Types of Healing Remedies

There are various types of natural healing remedies for each chakra. For example, there are animal totems that you can meditate on or carry small sculptures of with you. There are also incense and aromas, herbs, elemental associations, angels, essential oils, flowers, food and drink, sound frequencies, natural experiences, and sacred vowel sounds associated with each chakra. In the following sections, you are going to learn more about each one.

Animal Totems

Animal totems are specific animals associated with each of the chakras. You can use animal totems either by meditating on them, watching them in the wild, or carrying around a symbol of the animal with you.

The Root Chakra: Elephant, Snake, Ox, Bull, and Mole

The Sacral Chakra: Alligator or Crocodile, Fish, Dolphin, Sea Creatures and Water Animals, Elephant, Stag, and Badger

The Solar Plexus Chakra: Bear, lion, ram, and birds

The Heart Chakra: Black Antelope, Birds, Gazelle, Dove, Wolves, and virtually all mammals.

The Throat Chakra: Lions, White Elephants, and Bulls.

The Third Eye Chakra: Owl, Spirit Guides, Ancestors, Mountain Lion, Eagle, Butterfly and Black Antelope.

The Crown Chakra: Eggs, no specific animals are really associated with this chakra.

Incense and Aromas

When you are working with specific chakras, you may want to use incense or certain aromas to assist you. You can burn incense or light candles that have those specific scents. When you do, keep them nearby for you to smell and use. This will assist you in working with each specific chakra.

The Root Chakra: Myrrh, Vetiver, Sandalwood, Patchouli, Lavender, Clove, Cedarwood, Rosemary, and Cedar.

The Sacral Chakra: Sandalwood and Gardenia.

The Solar Plexus Chakra: Carnation.

The Heart Chakra: Jasmine and Lavender.

The Throat Chakra: Frankincense.

The Third Eye Chakra: Eucalyptus and Mugwort.

The Crown Chakra: Lavender, Juniper, Lotus and Sage.

Herbs

Working with herbs can be done either by drinking them as a steeped tea, eating them, or carrying them around with you in a medicine bag. Depending on the herb, there are many ways to use them or ingest them. You should always be mindful about what you are ingesting to ensure that you are not taking anything that you shouldn't be.

The Root Chakra: Burdock Root, Paprika, Cayenne Pepper, Dandelion, and all roots and herbs and spices that have an Earthy taste.

The Sacral Chakra: Fennel, Coriander, Cinnamon, Licorice, Vanilla, Caraway Seeds, Sesame Seeds, and all herbs and spices that have the ability to awaken and excite your senses and sensuality. Anything that assists you in benefiting your reproductive organs.

The Solar Plexus Chakra: Cinnamon, Ginger, Anise, Turmeric, Mint, Fennel, all herbs that are known to assist with the function of the liver and digestion systems.

The Heart Chakra: Marjoram, Basil, Cayenne, Rosemary, Thyme, Parsley, Sage, and any spices that have known benefits to the heart and the blood.

The Throat Chakra: Peppermint, Coltsfoot, Sage, Lemongrass, Salt, and all herbs and spices that are known to heal the throat and the vocal cords.

The Third Eye Chakra: Juniper, Eyebright, Mugwort, Lavender, Poppy, and all herbs and spices that are known for their benefit of assisting with eyesight, calming your nerves, or awakening your senses.

The Crown Chakra: Lavender, Gotu Kola, Sage, Lotus Flower, Basil, All-Spice, and all herbs that are considered to be sacred and known for the ability to benefit spirituality, cleansing, energizing and healing.

Elemental Associations

Life is comprised of five elements, and each chakra is associated with one of the five elements. When you are working with the elements, you can do it in a number of ways. For example, with Earth you can garden or walk on soil, for water you can bathe, swim or drink it, for air you can stand outside in a wind storm, for fire you may wish to light a candle, and with spirit you can meditate.

The Root Chakra: Earth

The Sacral Chakra: Water

The Solar Plexus Chakra: Fire

The Heart Chakra: Air

The Throat Chakra: Sound and Ether

The Third Eye Chakra: Light and Inner Sound

The Crown Chakra: Thought and All Other Elements

Angels

There are a number of angels and ascended masters and each chakra has its own angel that you can talk to or meditate on to gain assistance with a specific chakra or need. To work with angels you can talk to them, say affirmations, invoke them or pray to them.

The Root Chakra: Archangel Gabriel, and all angels of the Earth.

The Sacral Chakra: Zadkiel, and all angels that are associated with birth.

The Solar Plexus Chakra: Uriel, and all angels that are associated with peace.

The Heart Chakra: Raphael, and all angels that are associated with healing.

The Throat Chakra: Michael

The Third Eye Chakra: Chamuel, sometimes known as Camuel.

The Crown Chakra: Jophiel and Michael

Essential Oils

There are many ways to use essential oils, but typically you will diffuse them or rub them directly over the chakra. You may want to use a carrier oil depending on the oil. It is very important that you take the time to educate yourself on essential oils as there are varying things to consider. When you are not safe they can become dangerous, so it is important that you understand each oil and how you can use it and what the limitations are around it before you start to use it. This is the best way to prevent injury or illness.

The Root Chakra: Frankincense, Patchouli, Myrrh, Cedarwood, Ginger, Sandalwood, Vetiver, Cypress, Angelica, Benzoin, Oak Moss, Marjoram, and Rosewood.

The Sacral Chakra: Clary Sage, Bergamot, Jasmine, Geranium, Patchouli, Sandalwood, Orange, Rose, Cardamom, Ylang Ylang, Ginger, Cedarwood, Neroli, Rosemary, Patchouli, and Rosewood.

The Solar Plexus Chakra: Frankincense, Grapefruit, Geranium, Black Pepper, Juniper, Lemon and Lemon Grass, Rosemary, Sandalwood, Peppermint, Vetiver, Fennel, Bergamot, Cinnamon, Ginger, Clove, Chamomile, Lavender, Myrrh, Patchouli, Ylang

Ylang, Spearmint, Rose, Thyme, Mandarin, and Marjoram.

The Heart Chakra: Melissa, Jasmine, Geranium, Bergamot, Lavender, Rose, Neroli, Ylang Ylang, Chamomile, Sandalwood, Cypress, Eucalyptus, Lime, Mandarin, Lemon, Rosemary, Peppermint, Sweet Orange, and Tangerine.

The Throat Chakra: Cypress, Blue Chamomile, Geranium, Eucalyptus, Lavender, Myrrh, Spearmint, Peppermint, Tea Tree, Sandalwood, Hyssop, Bergamot, Jasmine, Roman Chamomile, Basil, Rosemary, Frankincense, Rosemary and Ylang Ylang.

The Third Eye Chakra: Cypress, Elimi, Clary Sage, Juniper, Marjoram, Rosemary, Rose, Frankincense, Lavender, Sandalwood, Lemongrass, Bay, Laurel, Helichrysum, Patchouli, Pine, Vetiver, and Thyme.

The Crown Chakra: Cedarwood, Frankincense, Benzoin, Lavender, Myrrh, Jasmine, Rose and

Rosewood, Neroli, Sandalwood, Elemi, Vetiver, Galbanum, and Spikenard.

Flowers

Flowers are a wonderful way to bring balance and harmony to your chakras. You can grow them or keep a bouquet on your table to gain benefits from the various flowers for each chakra.

The Root Chakra: Clematis, Rosemary, Cornflower, Amaryllis, Sunflower, and Daffodil.

The Sacral Chakra: Oak, Hibiscus, Elm, and Willow.

The Solar Plexus Chakra: Peppermint, Chamomile, Lemongrass, and Golden Yarrow.

The Heart Chakra: Poppy, Holly, Heather and Wild Rose.

The Throat Chakra: Trumpet Vine and Cosmos.

The Third Eye Chakra: Queen Anne's Lace and Wild Oats

The Crown Chakra: Tulip, Lotus, and Angelica.

Food and Drink

Eating and drinking things that are associated with your chakras are a wonderful way to balance them internally. This way allows you to balance them rather quickly and can be done easily. Ingesting is one of the easiest ways to absorb the benefits of your remedies.

The Root Chakra: All drinks and beverages that are dark red and brown in color. As well, anything that has an Earthy taste, especially root vegetables. Fresh ground coffee and all high protein foods also work.

The Sacral Chakra: Every food and drink that is orange in color, particularly those that are infused with citrus fruits. Any water, and every food that has a particularly high water content, such as cucumber, watermelon, and celery.

The Solar Plexus Chakra: All foods that are golden or yellow in color, including granola and grains. As well, any dairy products.

The Heart Chakra: All foods that are green in color, especially airy and leafy vegetables. As well, all warm foods and foods that are considered comfort foods are great foods for the heart chakra.

The Throat Chakra: All foods that are blue in color. Foods that are ethnic and exotic are also great for the throat chakra. As well, any fruits that grow on a tree or are citrus fruits. Soups and sauces as well as liquids and fruit juices are also great for this chakra.

The Third Eye Chakra: All foods that are indigo or purple in color, as well as dark cocoa and chocolate. As well, any food or drinks that are known to stimulate or assist in awakening your senses.

The Crown Chakra: All foods that are violet and white in color. Such as lavender, eggplant, and winterberries. As well, any other foods that are known to have benefits for cleansing and detoxing, energizing and spiritually enhancing someone.

Sound Frequencies

Each chakra has its own sound frequency. To activate the benefit of a sound frequency, simply turn it on and meditate to it.

The Root Chakra: 194.18 Hz, 396 Hz, and 256 Hz

The Sacral Chakra: 210.42 Hz, 417 Hz, and 384 Hz.

The Solar Plexus Chakra: 126.22 Hz, 528 Hz, and 320 Hz.

The Heart Chakra: 136.10 Hz, 639 Hz, and 341 Hz.

The Throat Chakra: 141.27 Hz, 741 Hz, and 341 Hz.

The Third Eye Chakra: 221.23 Hz, 852 Hz, and 448 Hz.

The Crown Chakra: 172.06 Hz, 963 Hz, and 480 Hz.

Natural Experiences

There are various natural experiences that you can have that will assist you in balancing your chakras. Each chakra has its own natural experience you can do in order to bring balance to it. You can often do these experiences quite easily, even from your own home. You do not need to do them for a lengthy period of time; however, you do want to do them long enough to absorb the benefit from them.

The Root Chakra: Walking barefoot on the Earth, as well as watching the sunrise or the sunset.

The Sacral Chakra: Sitting out in the moonlight and soaking it up, sitting next to or entering large open bodies of water.

The Solar Plexus Chakra: Soaking up fresh sunlight and being in the presence of sunflowers, particularly growing them.

The Heart Chakra: Spending time in nature that has been untouched by development and humankind, and spending time in a flower garden or specifically gardening in your own flower garden.

The Throat Chakra: Spending time underneath the clear blue sky or one with minimal and light fluffy clouds, as well as spending time next to the ocean.

The Third Eye Chakra: Spending time under the clear night sky, or any night sky if the sky is not clear for you. Star gazing is an especially powerful way to connect with this chakra.

The Crown Chakra: Spending time at the tops of mountains or gazing at the tops of mountains is a great way to connect with the Crown Chakra.

Sacred Vowel Sounds

To activate sacred vowel sounds, simply say the sound out loud. You can draw it out as though you were saying "ohm" and carry it for as long as you can. Doing so can bring balance and harmony to each of the chakras, depending on which one you desire to activate. Some even desire to use these sacred vowels during meditation to simply balance the chakras on a daily basis, as it is a gentle and easy way to harmonize them.

The Root Chakra: "Uh"

The Sacral Chakra: "Uu" (pronounced "you")

The Solar Plexus Chakra: "Oh"

The Heart Chakra: "Ah"

The Throat Chakra: "Ii" (pronounced "eye")

The Third Eye Chakra: "Aa" (pronounced "aye")

The Crown Chakra: "Ee"

As you can see, there are many ways that you can connect specifically with a chakra. You can use these methods or mix any number of the methods together in order to create a powerful healing ritual. When you are working on one specific chakra, you are going to want to do so either because you want to specifically heal that chakra or because you want to activate something that the chakra has to offer. For example, perhaps you want to interact more with your Crown Chakra to gain a greater connection with spirit for an intended purpose. You can then use the natural remedies within' this chapter to assist you in connecting with this chakra.

Conclusion

The chakras are energy centers that are located along the spine in your body. They are not physical beings but rather general locations where certain energies are drawn to. Each chakra has its own set of feelings, behaviors, emotions, organs and other things associated with it. You can identify chakras by their location and their color. There are seven in total and they stretch from the bottom of your tailbone to the top of your head.

When the chakras are unbalanced, your entire well-being is compromised. Underactive and overactive chakras can lead to a number of emotional, mental, spiritual and physical ailments. Initially, they may start out as a small concern but when you ignore the needs of the chakra for too long it can evolve into something much worse. To prevent yourself from suffering with the ailments that can be associated with unmaintained chakras, you should ensure that you spend time each day balancing them. There are many ways you can balance them, but meditation and crystals are the most common everyday choices.

If you are experiencing particular ailments or are struggling with a specific chakra, you may wish to take some time to heal that chakra specifically. There are many natural healing remedies that you can use with your chakras, and you may wish to combine them in order to gain the maximum value in bringing that chakra back into balance. Alternatively, some people enjoy spending a longer period of time bringing all of their chakras back into balance using these natural healing remedies. This is often something that people do when they are feeling completely unaligned and need to spend some time on themselves and bringing themselves back into their energetic powerhouse.

When you are working with your chakras, the best thing to do is take your time and develop a sort of relationship with them. When you do, you become more intuitive about each chakra and you will be able to quickly identify when one is unwell or out of balance. Then, you will be able to act fast and bring it back into balance quickly in order to keep it from causing you any excessive discomfort. When you do this, you also give yourself the opportunity to learn which balancing and remedial benefits work best for you. It does vary from person to person, so you will want to really pay attention to what you use that works best. You may even want to journal it so you can keep track.

In addition, you will find that each specific remedy and balancing tool has a specific purpose. Although it may work together with a certain chakra, some have different meanings from the others. For example, garnet is a wonderful grounding stone and black obsidian is a great protection stone. Both, however, are associated with the root chakra. When you are working with specific ailments or needs, there are almost always things that you can use that are specifically intended towards that need or ailment.

When you are choosing, you can choose intuitively or based on specific needs. Either will work well, so make the choice based on what is most appropriate to your present situation. If you are truly unsure about what you need, let your intuition guide you and see where it takes you. Often, it will bring you to exactly where you need to be with exactly everything that you need to have in order to take care of yourself.

I hope that this book was able to assist you in working with understanding your chakras and learning how you can effectively work with them. Each chapter was intended to assist you in gaining a greater understanding on your chakras, balancing and maintenance methods and healing options. I hope that you were able to learn all that you needed to in order to become a master of your own chakras.

The next step is for you to continue cultivating your relationship with your chakras and spending time every single day taking care of them and ensuring that they are balanced. Just as you would spend time eating and drinking to nourish your body and sleeping to keep yourself rested, you should spend time aligning your chakras to ensure that they are functioning optimally as well.

Thank you, and I wish you great luck in mastering your chakras.

Made in the USA
San Bernardino, CA
27 July 2018